SEARCHING FOR FANNIE QUIGLEY

SEARCHING FOR

Fannie Quigley

A Wilderness Life in the Shadow of Mount McKinley

JANE G. HAIGH

Jane G. Haigh

Swallow Press / Ohio University Press • Athens

Swallow Press / Ohio University Press, Athens, Ohio 45701
www.ohio.edu/oupress

Frontispiece: Fannie Quigley, 1923. *Photograph by Stephen Capps.*
UAF Stephen Capps Collection 83-149-2373

15 14 13 12 11 10   5 4 3 2

Library of Congress Cataloging-in-Publication Data

Haigh, Jane G.
  Searching for Fannie Quigley : a wilderness life in the shadow of Mount McKinley
/ Jane G. Haigh.
     p. cm.
  Includes bibliographical references and index.
  ISBN-13: 978-0-8040-1096-2 (hard cover : alk. paper)
  ISBN-10: 0-8040-1096-X (hard cover : alk. paper)
  ISBN-13: 978-0-8040-1097-9 (pbk. : alk. paper)
  ISBN-10: 0-8040-1097-8 (pbk. : alk. paper)
   1. Quigley, Fannie, 1871–1944. 2. Women pioneers—Alaska—McKinley, Mount,
Region—Biography. 3. Pioneers—Alaska—McKinley, Mount, Region—Biogra-
phy. 4. Gold miners—Alaska—McKinley, Mount, Region—Biography. 5. Frontier
and pioneer life—Alaska—McKinley, Mount, Region. 6. McKinley, Mount, Region
(Alaska)—Biography. 7. McKinley, Mount, Region (Alaska)—Social life and customs. 8. McKinley, Mount, Region (Alaska)—Gold discoveries. 9. Kantishna River
Region (Alaska)—Biography. 10. Kantishna River Region (Alaska)—Gold discoveries. I. Title.

F912.M2H35 2007
979.8'04092—dc22
[B]
                                                              2007000010

Alaska is a place where the personal response
to the land is part of what the land is. . . .
Writers who do not take adequate account
of this may get the details right but will
miss the spirit of the place entirely.

—*Chip Brown*

For Jane Williams and Ginny Wood,

and in memory of Liz Berry,

Celia Hunter, and Nina Mollett,

Alaska pioneer women all.

CONTENTS

—⟋⟋—

ACKNOWLEDGMENTS

So many people have helped me over the many years that I have been work-
ing on this project. First I would like to thank my editors at Swallow Press,
Gillian Berchowitz and Nancy Basmajian, and copyeditor Joan Sherman.
In no particular order, I thank Rick and Lissa Yoder and Deb Playfair, in
Nebraska; Jo Antonson; Jane Bryant, cultural resources specialist at Denali
National Park; Jane Williams, for perennial encouragement; Denali Backcountry Lodge; John Cook and associates at the Bureau of Land Management, whose index to the *Fairbanks Daily News-Miner* was invaluable for
the later period studied here, and Tom Walker, who shared his copy with
me; Mike Burwell, for the articles on "the widow Wilson"; Chuck Hawley,
for directing me to the memoirs of Ira Joraleman; Candy Waugaman, for
general all-around support as well as leading me to Lois McGarvey's memoirs in particular; Phyllis Movius, for sharing her work on Mary Lee Davis;
Diane Brenner, former archivist at the Anchorage Museum of History and
Art; Bruce Merrell at the Loussac Library, Alaska Collection; all those at the
University of Alaska Fairbanks Rasmuson Library, Arctic and Polar Regions
Archives, including Susan Grigg, Gretchen Lake, Richard Veazey, Ron In-
ouye, Rose Speranza, Bill Schneider, and Rene Blahuta, who was at the
archives when I started this project; National Park Service Historian Emeri-
tus William E. Brown, who was on the same track when I started and whose
work I have consulted since; Karen Anderson and Katherine Morrissey, for
expanding my horizons; Harry, Velma, and Amy Galblum, who read early
and often; Claire Rudolf Murphy, who also taught me to write along the
way; Ginny Wood; and the late Celia Hunter.

I started research on a short history of Denali National Park in 1986,
when my daughter Anna was four and her sister Molly just six months old.
After two or three years, it became clear that because the history of the park
and the climbers drawn to it was so interesting, my version of it would
never be short, and furthermore, the topic was already being pursued by
others. But very little was known about Fannie, and much of what had been

written about her was conflicting or just plain wrong. Thus began the search for Fannie Quigley. On our first trip to Kantishna and Quigley Ridge, I carried Molly in a backpack and my husband piggybacked Anna up the steep parts. It is hard to believe that as I finish this, Anna is graduating from college and has become a most able writer herself, as well as my best editor. So thanks especially to Molly, who truly grew up with this project; to my ever patient husband, Chris Haigh; and to Anna, who grew up with trips to Dawson and Kantishna and then went to college, became a writer, and helped me as an editor.

INTRODUCTION

Fannie Quigley became a legend in the Kantishna country, a mining district located at what is now the end of the Denali National Park Road. She arrived in the area in 1905 and stayed until she died alone in her cabin in 1944 at the age of seventy-four. She staked her share of mining claims and actually mined them; she also learned to hunt caribou, sheep, and moose and to trap fox, wolves, wolverine, and at least one lynx. She was famous for her wilderness cooking, including her flaky piecrusts made from rendered bear lard. She grew remarkable gardens full of vegetables and even many flowers on rocky slopes above tree line. And of course, there was her potato beer.

In the early years of the twentieth century, Mount McKinley was the object of intense interest among explorers from the eastern United States, many of whom were also striving to conquer the North and South Poles and other remote spots on the globe. A total of nine expeditions to the mountain's peak between 1903 and 1913 resulted in nearly a dozen books and countless articles in magazines of the day, such as *Outing, Scribner's,* and *National Geographic.*

Fannie's story first attracted me as I read about her during the course of research on the history of Mount McKinley National Park (now called Denali National Park and Preserve). At the University of Alaska Fairbanks, digging in the Francis P. Farquhar Collection of materials on the early climbers, I came across a yellowing magazine article from 1913, which turned out to be Fannie's first appearance in print: a piece in *Outing Magazine*. The author, climber and artist Belmore Browne, had written a series of five articles about his adventurous attempt on Mount

Fannie's cabin and garden on Quigley Ridge in the Kantishna. *UAF Fannie Quigley Collection 80-46-283*

McKinley in 1912. Heading back to civilization, he and his party had stopped at Fannie's for dinner. Calling her "one of the most remarkable women I have ever met," Browne gave this description of the then forty-three-year-old Fannie:

> Of medium height, her body had the strength and ruggedness of a man's. Below her short skirt came the leather of her rubber shoe packs and a flannel shirt covered her strong shoulders. But the most striking part of her were her keen, humorous eyes.
>
> She lived the wild life as the men did, and was as much at home in the open with a rifle as a city woman is on a city avenue, and she could not only follow and hunt successfully the wild game of the region, but could do a man's share in packing the meat to camp. From a physical standpoint she was a living example of what nature had intended a woman to be, and furthermore, while having the ability to do a man's work, she also enjoyed the life as a man does.[1]

Clearly breaking the mold on expectations for women of her own era, Fannie set an example for the modern wilderness women who would follow her into Denali National Park. Here was certainly an interesting character! Yet it was the caption on the photograph accompanying Browne's article that particularly grabbed my attention: "Mother McKenzie's Cabin." Who, I wondered, was Mother McKenzie?

Many popular articles have been written about Fannie, and the next thing I read was a story by Grant Pearson, a former Mount McKinley National Park superintendent, in an old *Alaska Sportsman Magazine*. The quintessential, mythical Fannie as presented by Pearson was a composite of all the stories that have come to be associated with her: how she arrived with her husband, Joe, a prospector; how she was known for her hunting and wilderness skills and her wild-game cooking; and how she had trudged up across the Chilkoot Trail back in 1898 and earned the nickname "Fannie the Hike" in the Klondike. Pearson clearly affirmed the fact that Fannie had been married to Joe when she arrived in Kantishna.

Because the genealogists' club in Fairbanks had made an index to obituaries in the *Fairbanks Daily News-Miner*, I was easily able to find Fannie's obituary, printed on Monday, August 28, 1944. It summed up everything about her that had been printed previously or was known at the time, which would be accepted as fact for the next fifty years. "One of Alaska's most colorful pioneers came to the end of her tread last week," it began, "when

Fannie Quigley died quietly and alone in her little house in the Kantishna where hundreds of park visitors, explorers, scientists, trappers and prospectors had visited her in the past 30-odd years since she settled there at the edge of McKinley National Park, a hundred miles from the railroad." The obituary ran through such facts as there were succinctly: "Born in Wahoo, Nebraska, March 18, 1871," she "ran away from her Bohemian home at an early age, learned to speak English while working her way westward along the railroad, and took up the trail of gold with the stampede to the Klondike in 1898." And then there came the kicker: "Many remember her place on No. 3 Above on Hunker Creek, and her marriage to Angus McKenzie in 1901."[2]

At least I had the answer to the "Mrs. McKenzie" question. But by the late 1940s, it seemed that no one who wrote about Fannie remembered her marriage to Angus. Grant Pearson had not mentioned it. Nor had he mentioned that Joe and Fannie had been divorced seven years before her death. In fact, in his account of Fannie's later years, he had stated (erroneously) that Joe was dead. But what had happened to the marriage to Angus? And when did Fannie really marry Joe?

Whenever I asked the local pioneer women about her, they looked askance, dismissed her, or simply giggled. It took me a while to figure out that she was one of those characters who, though beloved, was also endowed with some earthy characteristics: to put it plainly, she was loud, obstreperous, never spoke without swearing, and had a drinking problem. Finally, someone gave me a copy of Mary Lee Davis's book *We Are Alaskans*. Davis, a Wellesley graduate who visited Fannie in 1921, put a colorful spin on things when she noted that "her language was fairly Shakespearean in its rugged raciness."[3]

The newspaper obituary continued with a report of the funeral given for Fannie by her fellow Pioneer Women of Alaska: "And thus she was given up to immortal legend, for so long as there is an Alaska, stories will be told and retold with gusto and admiration for the lively mite of a woman whose famed personality, salty vigor, and great kindness are heart and sinew of the last frontier."[4]

Indeed, Fannie has become an "immortal legend." The stories have become a text, a narrative that repeats itself like a standard canon: "The Time She Shot the Two Caribou," "The Moose in the Middle of the River," "Crawling inside the Caribou Carcass," "Sewing Joe's Nose."

But what of the real woman behind the legend? Even the facts of her life, taken mostly from the obituary or from stories Fannie herself told to friends, have assumed a mythological status: "Leaving Home at an Early Age," "Working Her Way West on the Railroad," "Dance Hall Girl," "Fannie the Hike," "Meals for Sale." The myth of Fannie Quigley has inspired articles, stories, poetry, music, and plays. Was any of it true?

In short, I was intrigued, I was confused, and I was hooked. But there was a problem. I came suddenly to the realization that in spite of all that had been written, *no one even knew her name.* Without a maiden name to attach to the legend, details about her family, why she went north, or why she stayed for nearly forty years in her home in the high hills near Mount McKinley remained obscured by the tall-tale quality of the stories surrounding her.

Modern historians have access to a variety of resources, such as census data, mining claim records, newspaper indexes, court records, and city directories. But no information about Fannie's early life was accessible without that crucial piece of information—her maiden name, her birth name. Without that name or the background it would reveal, Fannie would remain a prisoner of her mythological status, presented as a symbol of the greater myth of the frontier.

Finding a maiden name became the crucial task. The marriage to Angus McKenzie was, I believed, the key, and so I wrote to the Yukon Office of Vital Statistics. My hand trembled as I opened the government envelope that came back a few weeks later—and not just because it was below zero as I checked my rural delivery box. The Yukon officials would not send a copy of the marriage certificate, but they did supply the information on it: "Fannie Sedlacek," the letter read, "daughter of J. and Josephine Sedlacek of Wahoo, Nebraska was married to Angus McKenzie, of Bruce, Ontario, Canada on October 1, 1900."[5] So there it was, a key that would unlock homestead records, census records, a past.

OBITUARY

—ɱ—

F. Quigley Found Dead by Friend

Famous Kantishna Woman Dies in Sleep after Long Career in North

One of Alaska's most colorful pioneers came to the end of her tread last week when Fannie Quigley died quietly and alone in her little house in the Kantishna where hundreds of park visitors, explorers, scientists, trappers and prospectors had visited her in the past 30-odd years since she settled there at the edge of McKinley National Park, a hundred miles from the railroad.[1]

Fannie was found dead Friday by her close friend and neighbor, Johnny Busia, who accompanied her body to Fairbanks yesterday to help make funeral arrangements. Busia said he had last visited the Quigley house on Tuesday and that it appeared Fannie had died that evening after he returned home.

BUSY AS USUAL

Busy as usual, Fannie was starting to pile some wood when he was there Tuesday, Busia said. When he made his second call Friday she lay on the couch dead, the wood still unpiled and a cook stove fire laid in the kitchen stove but not lighted. He deduced that she had laid down to rest before cooking her evening meal and had died in her sleep.

Thus ended the 73-year career of Fannie Quigley, the Midwestern girl who ran away from her Bohemian home at an early age, learned to speak English while working her way westward along the railroad, and took up the trail of gold with the stampede to the Klondike in 1898.

Fannie was born in Wahoo, Nebraska, March 18, 1871, in a settlement where little English was spoken but where she learned the art of gorgeous embroidery that helped her while away many a long winter hours in the north. Her journey westward was punctuated with several restaurant jobs and it was as a roadhouse operator that she was known in the Dawson

Country in '98. Many remember her place on No. 3 Above on Hunker Creek and her marriage to Angus McKenzie in 1901.

When gold started the stampede to Fairbanks shortly afterward, Fannie and her husband followed, stopping first at Chena where the original Tanana settlement was made, and following the population to Fairbanks.

In 1906, the new diggings in the Kantishna attracted Fannie and she again pulled up stakes, this time for the last time. With Joe Quigley she staked claims on Glacier and Caribou creeks and later a piece on Eureka creek. Fannie and Joe were married after that and prospected, mined, trapped and hunted together until they were divorced seven years ago. Joe now lives in Seattle.

WORKED LIKE MAN

In the Kantishna Fannie became a legend. Her abilities to work like a man, hunt, kill, skin, butcher, pack and cache her own game, embroider like an artist and entertain like a queen, spread her fame in books and stories and brought many visitors to her place in the shadow of Mt. McKinley to see and talk with the little woman who stood hardly five feet tall in her rough men's clothes.

With no formal education, Fannie all her life kept studying, collecting facts and ideas from newspapers, magazines, visitors, the radio, and her own observation of nature and people. Some of her game trophies have been preserved in museums and many of her sayings have been quoted by writers.

EXPERT GARDENER

In addition to her spectacular abilities on the sled-trail and the game trail, Fannie was also an expert gardener, a grower of fine vegetables for food as well as fine flowers for decoration. A selection of her finest pansies and other flowers she pressed in books and later reproduced in embroidery work on a beautiful tablecloth on which she spent many years and which was still unfinished at her death.

Fannie's ability as a seamstress got a real test many years ago when she got out her needle and made repairs on Joe Quigley's face after his nose was nearly torn off in the crack-up that followed the first airplane landing on Moose Creek near their diggings. The story is told with gusto by Fannie's friends as they escort visitors to the little frame house that Fannie and

Johnny Busia put up four years ago down the hill from the Red Top mine where she lived with a big tomcat for a companion.

Fannie continued to live in the Kantishna by choice, long after the normal time to retire to the easier life in civilization. Her industrious habits, her success as a miner and her ability to live mostly off the country had long since assured her financial independence. One trip outside many years ago, and several jaunts to Fairbanks for supplies and medical attention, including one siege in the hospital with a broken leg, always found her glad to return home to the Kantishna where there was no need to lower her high, ringing voice to conversational tones, or to forsake her outdoor garb.

Years ago Fannie wound up her business affairs, and her will reveals that she is survived by two sisters and three nieces.[1]

ABBREVIATIONS

ASL   Alaska State Library, Juneau, Alaska

FDNM   *Fairbanks Daily News-Miner*

NPS-DENA   Archives at Denali National Park, Denali Park, Alaska

NSHS   Library and Archives, Nebraska State Historical Society,
                Lincoln, Nebraska

UAF   Alaska and Polar Regions Archives, Rasmuson Library,
                University of Alaska Fairbanks

USGS-APU   U.S. Geological Service Archives at Alaska Pacific
                University, Anchorage, Alaska

YA   Yukon Archives, Whitehorse, Yukon Territory

ONE
〰

Nebraska and the West

Nebraska was often in the press in the late nineteenth century; the
name itself evoked a mental image of adventure, physical prowess,
and victory of man against the elements.
—Dorothy Creighton, *Nebraska, a History*

FANNIE QUIGLEY HAS BEEN THE EXEMPLAR of the pioneer spirit and wilderness lifestyle in Denali National Park, defying everything we thought we knew about the North as a story about man against nature. Much has been written about her, but few sources have had anything to say about where she came from or how she grew into the crusty old wilderness character who wore rough men's clothes and swore loudly. I decided to start at the beginning. I went to the public library and checked out the first book I found on Fannie's home state, Nebraska, which turned out to be a bicentennial history by Dorothy Creighton. Imagine my surprise to find that many of the qualities Fannie became famous for as an Alaskan pioneer could be attributed to her Nebraska upbringing. In the 1870s, it was the Nebraska frontier that was known for the "hairbreadth struggles of man against nature." Discussing "the Nebraska Psyche," Creighton attributed to Nebraskans "grit and determination, . . . audacity tempered with caution . . . the friendliness and generosity that makes no man a stranger on the prairie . . . and indomitable vigor transposed into emotional psychological and physical factors."[1] Of course, these are the qualities that all Alaskans claim as an integral part of the specifically Alaskan pioneering spirit, what they have been fond of describing as the myth and magic of the "last frontier." From her upbringing on a Bohemian homestead in Nebraska, Fannie developed the very qualities for which she would be known as an Alaska wilderness pioneer, including her perseverance, her audaciousness, her giving spirit, and the generous hospitality she offered to all who visited her. The hardships Fannie endured as a child on the Nebraska homestead enabled her to look with equanimity at the later hardships she faced at remote gold strikes in the Klondike and in the Kantishna. The homestead skills of gardening, wilderness cooking, and gathering wild foods would serve her well throughout her life.

Fannie's obituary had mentioned Wahoo, so on a map of Nebraska, I found the town in Saunders County and contacted the local historical society. Not surprisingly, Deb Playfair, the curator, had heard of Fannie Quigley. Many vacationing Nebraskans who took in the McKinley Chalet Dinner Theater's "Fannie Quigley Cabin Nite" returned home to ask about the famous Alaska pioneer. But of course, without a maiden name, there was little new information to be found. After I found her maiden name on the Dawson City marriage certificate and especially the names of her parents, I felt that anything was possible. It seemed like only a few days later when I walked down my snowy driveway in Fairbanks to find a letter from Saunders County: as always, I was excited by the prospect of receiving a new piece of information, a new clue in the mystery I was hoping to unravel. In the county courthouse, Deb had located the original homestead record, and she sent me a map of Saunders County marked with the distinct grid of the section lines; a red dot highlighted the Sedlaceks' homestead. I was suddenly consumed with a desire to see the site for myself. As much as I had read about Fannie, I could not really imagine Nebraska. Unsure just what I hoped to find there, I called friends who had moved to that state from Alaska and arranged a trip. I flew across the country at night, and east to Nebraska. As I drove south from the Omaha airport to my friends Rick and Lissa's farm, it was so dark the stars seemed close enough to touch; even the high beams of the headlights on my rented car seemed to be absorbed by the darkness of the gravel road bordered by pasture and cornfields. Finally, lights twinkled out of the windows of their large, old brick house, a bit off the road, near a typically small crossroads town just a few miles from the Missouri River.

The next morning, I set out to find Wahoo, driving west from the farm and the Missouri River. The land changed from high and flat plains to rolling hills, to low bottomlands in the floodplain of the Platte River, and back again to high, flat plains. But the farms and the towns went on and on. The towns were spread evenly over the countryside, mostly one to a section every 6 miles or so along roads that traced the regular grid of the section lines. (A township, the basic unit of survey, is 6 miles square and subdivided into thirty-six sections of 1 square mile each.)

Saunders County, bordered on the north and east by a wide bend in the Platte River and only some 40 miles from the Missouri at Omaha, was one

of the most populous counties in the state's early years. In 1870, Wahoo was the only town in the newly settled county, and it consisted of just one large and one small building.[2] When I arrived, Wahoo was a substantial county seat with an imposing courthouse on a rise in the center of town, and the Historical Society Museum was just below the hill near the railroad tracks. I stopped in to meet Deb Playfair and get directions to the farm.

The "Homestead Patent Record" showed that Vencil Sedlacek had claimed the "West Half of the North East Quarter of Section Two, in Township 14, Range Five East, containing 79 acres." Vencil settled a tract bordering a small tributary that flowed east about 3 miles to join Wahoo Creek. Following Deb's directions from Wahoo, I headed west on Route 92 toward the rolling hill country settled by many of the immigrants from Bohemia, now one of the provinces of the Czech Republic—so many, in fact, that the area is locally known as the Bohemian Alps. The towns on the map have names such as Plasi and Prague (pronounced with a long *a*, to rhyme with *plague*).

Following the map with the red dot, marking the section lines, I searched for the West Half of the North East Quarter of Section Two. It took three tries to find what I believed to be the right spot. At first, I turned and headed south on Route 79, where I found a high knoll with a wonderful view of the rolling farmland and a cemetery marked by a fancy cast-iron arch with Czech lettering. Standing in the wind and the sun, looking out over fields and farmsteads, I tried to pronounce the names on the headstones and

One of the earliest known drawings of the area around Wahoo, Nebraska. Drawing of the Wauhoo (Wahoo) Valley, Nebraska. *NSHS* strained to hear the voices of these new citizens of the land—Bartek and Cepak, Hakela and Jelinek, Hurka, Machesek, Malesek and Maly, Pacula and Paseka, Pop, Rezak, Rehak and Sabatka, Siminek, Svoboda, Tomes and Tomisek. Was this high bluff really the homestead?

I pulled out the map again to verify my location, studied the section numbers, and realized that this windswept knoll could not, after all, be the right farm. So I drove back on Route 92 east, to the junction where Route 79 heads north. The farmstead on the southwest corner, with its small, un-kempt house and large trees, occupied another windswept hillside. Cars and farm equipment were scattered around the barn and a metal machine shed. I tried to imagine that the north-facing hillside above the creek might once have been a place for a dugout sod house. But the creek trended in the wrong direction, and a north-facing hillside would have been a cold choice. Studying the maps again, I realized that Route 92 was not, after all, on the township boundary. The boundary was actually one section to the north, so I set out again, going north on Route 79 toward Prague. A mile up the road, I found Wahoo Creek, flowing northeast, in the direction indicated on the map. Turning left a mile farther on, I followed a rutted dirt road through cornfields and woods until it crossed the creek on a bridge. Up the road from the bridge was a homestead with the name Pacula on the mailbox.

The farmsteads along the main road had been showy places, most of them occupying the crown of a hill with the houses facing the road and the barns arrayed to the side and out back. But this place was different. It was set off the road and down toward the creek in a hollow. I could not even see the house from the road. My heart beat faster and my palms turned clammy as I turned into the drive, passing the outbuildings. The house, painted turquoise and neat as a pin behind a picket fence, was tucked away down by the creek. This must be Vencil Sedlacek's original claim, I thought. I knocked on the door, but no one answered. To stay felt like trespassing, and so I left, passing a tree, by the creek, that was so big it could have been a hundred years old. It might even have been there when Fannie was a girl playing in the creek with her sisters, I mused. I could imagine that Vencil Sedlacek claimed the creek to get water for his family, the livestock, and the crops.

In the fading daylight, a soft sunset haze settled on the homestead, a low hollow in the prairie; a flock of birds stirred in the scrub brush by the creek. As I drove back to Wahoo, I had to remind myself that when Vencil and Mary Sedlacek arrived, there were no quaint farmhouses, no farm-steads with their windbreaks, no trees, no cropland plowed in even stripes across the hills, no fences, no rows of corn, no herds of cattle, none of the features we associate with the pastoral countryside. There was nothing then but the land. Just the prairie and the wind.

—⁓—

Later, I went to Lincoln to consult the census records. The 1870 census of Saunders County showed that twenty-five-year-old Vencil, listed by the anglicized name James, was a farmer in Township 14. He and twenty-one-year-old Josephine were the parents of a daughter, age two, born in Iowa, and a new baby, Frances, later known to all as Fannie; she was six months old at the time, her month of birth listed as March.[3] Surrounding their homestead were thirteen more families from Bohemia, and others from Ohio, Iowa, Indiana, Kentucky, Illinois, New York, Wisconsin, Pennsylvania, and England. Nearby townships were populated by Swedes, near the settlement of Malmo, as well as Finns, Germans, and Russians.

The Sedlaceks' journey began to make sense after I found a copy of Rose Rosicky's *History of Czechs in Nebraska*. Sedlacek is a common family

Census record, Saunders County, Nebraska, Township 14, Range 5, showing that Fannie was born in 1870.

		Name	Age	Sex	Color	Occupation	Real estate	Personal	Birthplace
		— Dorotha	40	F	"	Keeping House			Bohem
		— George	1	M	"				Nebra
501	496	Souharare Mathias	27	M	W	Farmer	300	150	Bohem
		— Mary	19	F	"	Keeping House			Bohem
		— Thomas	1	M	"				Nebra
502	497	Frank Antone	55	M	W	Farmer	300		Bohem
503	498	Selarik Jamey	25	M	W	Farmer	300		Bohem
		— Josephine	21	F	"	Keeping House			Bohem
		— Josephine	2	F	"				Iowa
		— Frances	6/12	F	"				Nebra
504	499	Maller George	34	M	W	Farmer	200	200	Bohem
		— Mary	30	F	"	Keeping House			Bohem
		— James	6	M	"				Bohem
		— George	3	M	"				Bohem
		— Mary	1	F	"				Nebra
505	500	Ellingale George	34	M	W	Farmer	200	175	Bohem
		— Mary	30	F	"	Keeping House			Bohem
		— George	11	M	"				Bohem
		— Maline	9	F	"				Bohem

Vencil, Josephine, and Josephine Julia Sedlacek, ca. 1868. *Courtesy of the Oien family*

name in parts of Iowa today, taking up nearly a page of the Cedar Rapids phone book, and that is where Vencil Sedlacek, like many of his compatriots, first settled. But Iowa was already beginning to be settled up in those days, and the price of land was starting to rise. Peter Kastle was one of the first Bohemians to leave Iowa for Nebraska, taking up land in the western half of Saunders County, an area of rolling hills, with a network of streams cutting through low bottomlands supporting the only trees on the open plains.[4]

Bohemian immigrants were among those attracted to Nebraska's open lands and fertile soil. The Bohemians were known in Europe as a proud people who loved language and learning. The University of Prague was among the first in Europe, founded in 1348. Yet as a part of the Hapsburg Empire, they had been reduced to the empire's peasants in a country with too many people and too little land. By the nineteenth century, the major centers of Europe were all familiar with expatriate Bohemian families that had been expelled from the empire. A final attempt at revolution in 1848 began the modern exodus to the United States. Many of the immigrants rejected the Catholic faith, which had been imposed by the empire, and became free-thinkers.[5]

—⁊⁊—

Fannie's mother, Josephine, died in 1875 at the age of twenty-six, when Fannie was five, according to family records. Perhaps her death was the result of the frequent epidemics of diphtheria or typhus, or perhaps it occcured in childbirth. We will probably never know because, as local sources report, this was too early for death certificates, newspapers, or even church records. With three young daughters and a baby boy, Vencil was quick to find another wife. On January 27, 1876, at age thirty-one, he married another Bohemian immigrant, Mary Tomes, the twenty-one-year-old daughter of neighboring homesteaders. Mary bore two more children before 1880: Anna, in January 1878, and Victor, in 1879.[6]

What was Fannie's life like? With no memoirs and no written records, we must compile a composite picture from available materials, such as the oral histories in Rose Rosicky's *History of Czechs in Nebraska* and the novels and other fictional works that try to tell the story. Although our mental image of homesteading may include the warmth of the hearth, with family members working together taming the prairies, homesteading was, in reality, desperately difficult. It is not surprising that we have no account of Fannie's family experiences, for few who homesteaded had the time, education, or inclination to write about their daily struggles. And those who did were motivated to remember the good times or to chalk up the difficulties to character building. The first-person accounts of immigrant Bohemian homesteaders help us imagine what Fannie's family must have gone through. Survivors of the period recounted, in stark, spare narratives, their early experiences of privation and the hardships that greeted the settlers. Later, after life improved, people tended to look back through rose-colored glasses, minimizing the real suffering they endured. "We toiled hard and kept up our courage and now, when we have comfort and plenty, the past seems like a bad dream," said Joseph Krenek.[7]

Contrary to the pervasive mental image, I learned, the classic sod house was actually a later, more modern development. The earliest settlers carved out primitive dugouts, caves cut into hillsides and covered with pole roofs, like the structure pictured in a popular photograph at the Nebraska State Archives called "Our Home."

"Our Home." The abysmal dugout of an early homestead family was far more primitive than even the traditional sod house, which was a later development. *NSHS C689-45*

Fannie's father and other farmers of the early years were barely eking out a living. They were merely existing—subsisting off meager crops, holding onto the land, and doing whatever work was obtainable for trade, hoping for a miracle of weather or crops or work to inch ahead in what today we would call a Third World environment. Those who started in 1870 were met by a series of plagues that would rival the afflictions of the Old Testament: drought, financial panic, locusts, blizzards, dust storms, prairie fires, and drought again.

Nebraska author Bess Streeter Aldrich based her 1928 classic novel, *A Lantern in Her Hand,* on documentary materials and interviews conducted with the remaining original settlers. The book is revered in Nebraska; it is understood by Nebraskans as embodying a kind of collective truth that goes beyond dry facts to explain what these pioneering years were truly like.[8] Aldrich described farming in Nebraska in the 1870s through the experience of a fictional heroine, Abbie Deal, and her husband, Will, who settled in 1868. First, the virgin prairie had to be broken and corn planted in the roughly turned sod. But the first year's crop, the "sod-corn," was always meager, good only to feed to livestock on the stalks. Then, due to lack of rain, the crops of 1870 and 1871 were "only half a crop," and 1872 was just as bad. The winters brought raging blizzards and howling winds. But the year 1873 was worse yet, described, even amid these dire conditions, as "a low point."[9]

Despite the fact that the crops had not measured up to the hype of the area's promoters, the population of homestead farmers exploded across the plains in these early years as the railroads advertised for settlers and encouraged development. And as the railroads expanded, more bonds were floated for the already heavily indebted rail lines, decreasing their value and leading to an ever expanding market bubble. In 1873, the bubble burst, pricked by the failure of investment bankers J. Cook and Company. The panic of 1873 was very real for Nebraska farmers, who could only watch helplessly as prices fell for their corn and wheat crops. A bushel of corn worth thirty-two cents in 1870 when farmers optimistically broke their prairie homesteads was worth only half that in 1873. "The bottom of the market dropped out," wrote Aldrich, "and prices were so low that it did not even pay to haul the scanty crop to market."[10] The homesteaders burned their corncobs and twists of hay to keep warm.

This image of burning the corn and hay is one I found unforgettable after spending many long winter nights reading Laura Ingalls Wilder's stories to my daughters. Now, when I try to imagine Fannie's life on the plains as a little girl, I often think of images in the *Little House on the Prairie* series.

Wilder, born in 1867, was only three years older than Fannie, and her childhood experiences on the prairies and the plains from Wisconsin to Kansas, Minnesota, and South Dakota closely paralleled Fannie's. She and her family worked their way west, beginning anew three or four times before finally settling in the famous little house on the homestead in De Smet, South Dakota.

Optimism returned as farmers planted the crop of 1874, but that year brought the worst plague of all—grasshoppers. They appeared in July, coming from the west out of a bright summer sky, like a great glittering cloud: "In a clear hot July day a haze came over the sun. The haze deepened into a gray cloud. Suddenly the cloud resolved itself into billions of gray grasshoppers sweeping down upon the earth. The vibration of their wings filled the ear with a roaring sound like a rushing storm."[11]

The grasshoppers devastated the crops and the gardens and ate everything in sight. Then they burrowed into the ground to lay eggs, destined to hatch and repeat the devastation the following summer. That winter was one of nearly complete despair as the proud homesteaders, to their shame, were forced to rely on donated aid. Even the army participated in distributing surplus clothing and equipment. After the grasshopper devastation at the Ingallses' home in Wisconsin, Pa Ingalls had to leave home to find paying work harvesting crops. It was also during that period that Laura's sister Mary contracted a fever and was left blind. In spite of all efforts, the Ingalls family lost the Wisconsin land and moved farther west.

Like all their neighbors, the Czechs in Nebraska faced hard times, often coming close to starvation. "During the first two years there was so little food that we could not supply our needs," said Frank Cejda in his oral history collected by Rosicky, "barley coffee and corn mush, cooked in water, was our menu, . . . we had no cow to give us milk."[12] Anton Brazda's family's first home was a dugout on the side hill of someone else's claim. "Father and mother worked for the few farmers that were here, earning just enough to keep us children and grandfather from starving," he said. "While our parents were away, which was almost all the time, Grandfather looked after us and gathered sunflowers, gum weeds, and plum brushes for fuel, storing what he could gather for winter use."[13] One of the first luxuries was a cow, which cost the Brazda family five months of the father's labor. "After two years . . . Father started to earn his first cow . . . for which he gave some five months labor on a farm some twelve miles from our home." Then Brazda's father labored twelve months longer to earn two steers for their first team. Having started out in 1868, it took the family five years to cross the threshold of minor prosperity. By 1873, the father had gotten work constructing a courthouse. They were using money now and had a log house, a cow for milk and butter, and a team of oxen, and they had raised sufficient crops to sustain themselves.

In 1879, when Fannie was nine, Vencil proved up on the homestead and then sold it almost immediately. Like many homesteaders, he seems to have patented his land only so that he could immediately sell it to pay debts and have enough money to support the family.[14] It took money to sustain a family through early years of scanty crops. Yet even though the grasshopper plague abated in 1876 and a drought that had marked the beginning of the decade ended when rain came early in 1877, the farmers did not see the economic prosperity that was the promise of the new land. In fact, under the best of conditions, farming hardly paid its own way. There was a high cost to farming, and a settler needed a source of cash to develop a homestead. Farmers were forced to take on debt to finance seed and equipment for the coming year. With the end of the drought, prices for grain fell again, and indebted farmers lost their land to the banks. Smaller landholders sold out to those few who were willing to buy with borrowed money.[15] The most famous of all Nebraska writers, Willa Cather, used this scenario in her *O Pioneers!* in which her heroine is the one who buys the land from her less fortunate neighbors. Both this work and *My Ántonia* focus on the lives of Bohemian immigrants like the people Cather knew from her years in Red Cloud, Nebraska.

The census enumerator in June 1880 counted the Sedlacek family in Elk Precinct, near the Czech settlement of Plasi, not far from the original homestead. Vencil, now aged thirty-six, and his wife, Mary, aged twenty-six, were both farming. They had six children by then. The eldest, Josephine, aged twelve, was "keeping house" and caring for Joseph, age six, Anna, age two, and Victoria, age one. Frances, aged ten, however, was listed as attending school in 1880. Her sister Mary was eight. So with Josie old enough to take care of the younger children, two adults free to do the heavy farmwork, and money from the sale of the homestead, perhaps now the family was able to get ahead. Like many young women of this early period of homesteading, Mary, the young stepmother, could neither read nor write.[16] Although Fannie, as the second oldest, may have helped with gardening, cooking, and gathering wild foods from the prairies and fuel for heat, she was also able to go to school. Her obituary stated that Fannie "learned to speak English while working her way westward along the railroad," but it seems likely that she actually did attend school, conducted in English, for at least a few years. A school was established in a neighboring section, and the schools, established by the state, taught in English; according to school records, Fannie attended at least for 1880.[17] It seems, then, that even though Czech was her first language and the primary language spoken in her home, Fannie was at least exposed to English through one or more years of schooling.

The settlers certainly made use of whatever wild foods were available. Aldrich described picking wild grapes and wild plums and pie plant after the grasshopper plague.[18] "We subsisted on wild spinach leaves," Frank Cejda recounted. "For fuel we had to depend on sunflowers, cornstalks, weeds and straw." Cejda also described how the settlers used game. "Meat was scarce, and wild game also, for there was nothing for it to feed on. . . . When crops began to be raised, grouse, prairie chicken, deer and elk came. They disappeared late, when the country began to be more thickly settled. . . . After our first year or two, wild game provided us with meat, and hunting became a delight."[19] Many who grew up this way were only anxious to get this rugged life behind them and move into more civilized circumstances. But something about the life and the challenges it entailed must have appealed to Fannie, for she was to live this way for the rest of her life.

By 1885, the Sedlacek family had moved again, this time to farmland in Chapman Precinct, where they endured yet more hardship. Nebraska conducted its own census in 1885, and it also counted deaths for the year: the three youngest Sedlacek children—Joseph, Anna, and Victoria—are missing from the census list. Homesteading life on the prairie took a terrible toll on the young. Losing infants and children, many from diphtheria, was a common, grim fact of life. Of eighteen deaths in Chapman Precinct alone, thirteen were children; six were two and under. Ten of these children died of diphtheria, including four from one family, ages ten, eight, six, and four. The pattern was the same in nearby precincts, and it was probably diphtheria that took the three younger Sedlacek children.[20]

According to the 1885 census, Fannie, at fifteen, and her sister Mary, thirteen, were "at home," but neither was in school. Fannie's oldest sister, Josie, was seventeen and listed as a laborer. New members of the family were Vencil, two, a new Anna, one, and Theresa, aged six months. Through the other children's deaths and then the births of the three new children to Fannie's young stepmother, Fannie and her two full sisters must have carried much of the load of the household labor.

Vencil was one of only sixteen farmers in the precinct listed as "renting for a share," sharecropping on someone else's land because he had lost his own homestead. In addition to enumerating populations and counting deaths, this state census also counted farm production. Vencil seems to have given up on any dreams of prosperity or raising cash crops and instead was struggling to feed and maintain his family on a subsistence basis. He grew only 15 acres of corn, producing 500 bushels, and 1 acre of potatoes, producing only 125 pounds. The family livestock consisted of a few cows, seventeen pigs, and forty-five chickens. There was no estimated value of farm production, no cash crop. Vencil's acreage consisted of 56 acres of tilled land and 100 acres of pasture. Although better than the starvation and poverty of the earliest years, this was still a meager living for his growing family of eight.[21] The 1885 census was to be the last in which Fannie and her sisters Josephine and Mary were reported as living with the family.

By December 1890, Josephine had married and then divorced before marrying again a few years later.[22] Fannie, as the second oldest, was probably the next sent to "work out," or help support the family. Willa Cather's heroine Ántonia, like Fannie, was a Bohemian immigrant girl whose family was a part of the first wave of early settlement. Cather portrays a world where older girls were often hired out to other farms for the little cash the family required. As the second child, Fannie probably had to help her father in the fields: immigrant families could not afford to restrict girls to housework. Her father, stepmother, and the younger children (Vencil, Anna, and Theresa as well as George, who was born in 1886) moved to Custer County, farther west, where they—but not the three older girls—were counted by the 1890 census and where another child, John, was born that year.[23] Hard times undoubtedly continued for the family. The years between 1885 and 1887 had been a time of speculative boom in western Nebraska. Then came another drought and a bust to the boom, as many settlers left. By 1890, farmers were three years behind in their loans, and after 1890, there were numerous foreclosures as a result of the "cumulative force of hard times."[24]

In Cather's novel, many farm girls, including Ántonia and her friends, were hired out in domestic work, but others went to work in the primitive roadhouses or restaurants on the railroad lines. The scant evidence available suggests that, like them, Fannie started working as a cook or waitress for the construction crews on the rail lines. As her obituary stated, she "learned to speak English while working her way westward along the railroad," and "her journey westward was punctuated with several restaurant jobs."[25]

The miracle of microfilm at the Nebraska Historical Society in Lincoln allowed me to find the rest of the family's story. In the "underground census" of graveyards compiled by the good historians of Nebraska, I found the death date for Fannie's father, Vencil, in 1921. And from the date, I was able to go directly to the microfilm for the local paper, where I found the obituary. By 1902, the rest of the family had moved again, this time east from Custer County, just over the county line into the Bohemian settlement of Geranium, in Valley County. There, perhaps they finally found a measure of prosperity. The younger children, Anna, Theresa, and George, continued to live at home into the 1920s, and the younger Vencil, known as James, married and settled nearby with his own children.[26]

Most of Nebraska's counties and towns have their centennial histories, their county and town history books. But these have been written from the perspective of the pioneers or their descendants who still live in the locales. The town histories concentrate on the later period of town building, the era of farmstead building when the farmers were finally becoming successful and families were able to replace their sod houses with modern frame dwellings.[27] And in fact, many of the "pioneers" celebrated in Saunders County did not even arrive until after 1885. By that time, Fannie and her family were gone. Like apparitions on the prairie, their experiences in Saunders County were relics of the first years.

Between 1886 and 1889, Nebraska was enjoying a boom in railroad construction, with trunk and branch lines nearly doubling the railroad mileage in the state.[28] The Burlington Railroad was laying track for a branch line through Saunders County in 1886 and 1887. We can imagine that Fannie was a waitress or cook's helper in a company mess hall. When the local

Railroad graders above Sargent, Nebraska, 1889. If Fannie worked on the railroads through Nebraska, it would have been in the camp of a contractor, such as the transitory camp shown here, with many women accompanying the workers. *NSHS RG2608-PH:3496*

rail lines were completed around 1889, she moved west with the construction work.[29]

Like her immigrant family's life on the plains, Fannie's years with the railroads as they expanded westward are difficult to document, as are the stories of the many other young working women in the West. In railroad archives, there are sometimes lists of workers, but no women were employed directly by the rail companies. Instead, the official mess crews were employed by contractors. Thus, these women do not show up in records or statistics of railroad workers. I read through the 600-plus pages of Maury Klein's *Birth of the Union Pacific* and visited the official Union Pacific Museum in Omaha.[30] I asked at the Archives of the Nebraska State Historical Society in Lincoln. I studied hundreds of photos of railroad building and railroad workers. But no women were to be found. I located only two photos with mere glimpses of railroad camp restaurants.

In truth, this period of Fannie's life, between 1886 and 1898, is still largely a mystery. She remained close to her two full sisters, Josephine and Mary, for the rest of her life, and all three had headed west.[31] Nearly illiterate, Fannie probably did not write to her sisters during that period. Perhaps she was a waitress or cook's helper, as she told Mary Lee Davis years later in Alaska. Perhaps the truth was something else entirely, something that she never wanted to reveal. Whatever her occupation, Fannie became part of a large group of working single women in the West. These young women, descendants of Irish, Swedish, Norwegian, Czech, and German immigrants, made their own way in every western community. But their stories were never well documented. And once she had left, there was really no chance for Fannie to go home again.

Fannie as a young woman. *Courtesy of the Oien family*

TWO

Fannie the Hike

Dawson and the Klondike, 1898–1903

Fannie was 27 when she determined to follow the stampede to the Klondike
in 1898. For some reason she and Joe never ran across each other there. Fannie
earned her living first as a dance hall girl, later by operating eating places.

—Grant Pearson, *My Life of High Adventure*

FANNIE BEGAN LIFE IN THE KLONDIKE as a prospector on November 21, 1899,
when she obtained Free Miner's Certificate #45627, under the name of
Fannie Senlock, from the gold commissioner at Hunker Creek, entitling her
to stake her own claim. At the same time, she had a job working at a roadhouse on Hunker Creek.[1]

For ten years, Fannie had apparently "worked her way west" from Nebraska as a cook in railroad construction camps. As a single woman in the
West, she had not only learned to cook a camp meal but also picked up a
brand of English as spoken by Irish railroad workers, a dialect that included
mostly swear words. The ability to survive in a world full of men was not the
least of her accomplishments.

Twenty-seven-year-old Fannie Sedlacek was among the thousands of
workers in the West who heralded the news of the arrival of two treasure
ships from the Klondike in July 1897. Electrified with the news of "a ton of
gold on board," the crowd on hand to greet the *Portland* as it docked in Seattle, waiting to see the grizzled miners with their gold, must have been surprised to see another passenger disembark—Ethel Berry, quickly dubbed the
"Bride of the Klondike." Ethel had traveled to the North with her husband,
Clarence, in the spring of 1896, where they had been lucky enough to stake
one of the richest claims in the Klondike. Besieged by newspaper reporters,
she told her story over and over—giving hope and encouragement to thousands of women that this need not be seen as an opportunity for men only.

Fannie and many others heard Ethel Berry's stories of the terrible food
in the northern camps and of the miners who were too busy at the bottoms

of their mining shafts and too tired when they emerged to start the stoves and cook for themselves.[2] These women, experienced as camp and restaurant cooks, railroad and ranch cooks, became convinced that their traditionally female skills would be valued in that newly fabled region, a place where gold was said to be so plentiful that people could pick up nuggets off the ground. Fannie was among the thousands of women who would set out for the Klondike.[3]

Reeling from the continuing depression that had begun in 1893, tens of thousands of men and perhaps a few thousand women vowed to join the rush to the Klondike, and perhaps forty thousand actually reached Dawson City, the new boomtown on the Yukon. The scramble was on to purchase passage on one of the many wretchedly crowded ships ready to set sail up Alaska's Inside Passage for Skagway and Dyea, the jumping-off points for the trails to the Klondike.

Once on board a ship, a gold rusher had to choose between the two trails over the high passes into the interior and the lakes at the headwaters of the Yukon River. A common saying was that whichever trail you chose, you would wish you had taken the other. The more famous Chilkoot Trail heading up the Dyea (now Taiya) River from the Dyea Inlet was shorter and more direct. But with its infamous thirty-five-degree pitch leading to the summit, it could not be negotiated by pack animals; widely circulated photos showed hundreds of men climbing the snow-covered trail in lockstep. To circumvent this route, some entrepreneurs landed in the neighboring inlet, where the new town of Skagway was growing out of the forest at the beginning of the new White Pass Trail. Advertised as an easier route suitable for pack animals, it was, in reality, so treacherous that it soon became known as the Dead Horse Trail.

I never found a record documenting Fannie's actual crossing of the Chilkoot Trail, but I do have a photo of Fannie sitting astride a mule in front of a barn, whose name I cannot read, with a view of Skagway in the background. The dress and hat she wears are the same as in a photo she sent to one of her sisters. It is not much to go with.

Skagway appeared to new arrivals as the most lawless town on earth in the fall and winter of 1897–98, almost completely under the control of a con man named Jefferson Randolph "Soapy" Smith. Taking advantage of the newness of the town and the lack of any local government, Smith organized a protection racket with the aid of some of his cronies from Denver. The gang demanded payoffs from the saloons, gambling establishments, and prostitutes and seduced the more honest elements of the community with a promise to keep out truly violent criminals. The gang existed to fleece the thousands of travelers with con games, crooked gambling establishments, and fake businesses, such as the Telegraph Office (which had no telegraph line out), Reliable Packing, and the Information Office. Those who ran afoul of the gang could find themselves in trouble—or dead.[4]

Following fears of starvation in the winter of 1897–98, the Canadian government began to require those crossing the border into the Yukon to carry with them enough provisions to last for a year. These rations became the proverbial "ton of goods" that all Klondikers had to procure in Seattle or Victoria: hundreds of pounds of flour, sides of bacon, sacks of beans, crates of dried milk, dried apples and raisins, sugar, and molasses. Freighting this pile of goods over the pass was a daunting undertaking for men and women alike. Of course, women with money, such as Chicago socialite Martha Black or journalist Emma Kelly, could hire packing companies to carry their goods for them. But not everyone could afford this expenditure. Frequently, men and women organized themselves into informal companies to share the work of packing. Fifty-eight-year-old Anna DeGraf joined such a company, taking over the cooking chores for the group while the men packed the outfits themselves. The young boys in her group all called her "Mother," and she cooked for them and made sure they had dry socks. She earned the lifelong esteem of many a Klondiker by generously providing a simple meal at a time of need.[5]

Still other women scraped together the money for passage on a ship and then took jobs in Skagway, hoping to work their way to Dawson. Harriet Pullen, formerly the owner of a prosperous farm in Washington, contrived to bake apple pies from the mounds of dried apples that turned up as a part of many a gold seeker's outfit. Then she had her horses shipped up and worked as a packer, undoubtedly with a payoff to the gang. Harriet never bothered to go to Dawson at all, instead establishing her famous Pullen House Hotel right in Skagway. Mollie Walsh, who had been working at a laundry in Butte, found a series of restaurant jobs in Skagway and then opened a roadhouse in a tent at the top of the White Pass Trail. Here was an opportunity! On the trail itself, travelers and packers alike, frozen and half starved, were nearly desperate for a warm meal. Mollie befriended the packers, undoubtedly assuring her source of supplies, and moved on to Dawson when the trail finally melted out in the spring.[6]

Many other women were operating roadhouses and eating establishments at various places along the trails—Sheep Camp, the Scales, Lake Bennett, and White Pass City—during the height of the rush. Their testimony reveals that it was comparatively easy for a hardworking woman to find employment in Skagway, along the trail, or in Dawson.[7]

Of course, being a woman on the trail was not without its dangers or insults. There were prostitutes and pimps traveling as well. One woman on the Chilkoot Trail, en route to join her husband, was refused service at a roadhouse: the proprietor would not take a chance on her being a prostitute and would not relent until, by chance, an acquaintance of her husband's verified her story.

Peggy Shand traveled the trail with her husband as far as Lake Bennett, where they waited in vain for their goods to be delivered by the packer they had hired. When her husband was stricken by snow blindness, Peggy made the trip from Lake Bennett to the Scales at the bottom of the pass by herself, and on the way, she was accosted by a pimp who hoped to enlist her.[8]

While we do not have an actual account of Fannie's trip over the pass, from what we know of her personality, coupled with the experiences of others, we can imagine that she arrived in Skagway and worked her way over the trail. She probably had only enough money for her passage and thus did not outfit with the latest appurtenances available at the Hudson's Bay Company store in Victoria or the ton of goods from the dealers in Seattle. It is easy to imagine her as one of the unnamed women cooking or serving at one of the unnamed roadhouses along the way.

Skagway, from the east. Fannie sent this photo home to her sister, the only real evidence of her trip through Skagway. *Courtesy of the Oien family*

One of two known photos that show Fannie in a long black dress and prim hat. (The other photo, in which she is shown mounted on a mule, was found at her home in Kantishna after her death and is now in the UAF Fannie Quigley Collection.) She sent this photo to her sister, and it survived in the family's possession. *Courtesy of the Oien family*

It seems somehow fitting that, today, Skagway is once again filled with milling if disoriented crowds. Of course, most modern visitors to the city arrive on the cruise ships that have transformed southeast Alaska. I wonder if they can picture Skagway as the gold rushers first saw it: nothing but mudflats easing almost directly into the forest. Back then, crusty West Coast trader Captain William Moore had staked the site as a homestead, but by the end of August 1897, it had been overrun by the first gold seekers. They ignored Moore's claims and proceeded to lay out a town, with the wide main street, Broadway, running from the beach back through the forest to the beginning of the White Pass Trail. The fact that Moore's cabin was in the middle of a street seemed just an inconvenience. Those arriving in the fall of 1897 saw only a muddy swath where Broadway was supposed to be, lined with a variety of tents and hastily built storefronts.

Fannie's childhood of hardship on the Nebraska homestead and her experience cooking for crews of men on the railroads in the West had prepared her for life in the Yukon. She had somehow learned to take care of herself in a world of men, experience that would be more than useful in Dawson, where men outnumbered women by twenty to one.

Stories that say Fannie was a dance hall girl in Dawson for a time reinforce the idea that she arrived broke and perhaps took to the dance halls as a way to make her living through that first tumultuous winter. One Dawson City writer described this as a not uncommon fate: "Many good and virtuous girls who came to Dawson to seek honest work in order to better their impoverished condition from the slavish position they held elsewhere, braved to little purpose the heart-rending dangers which they nobly conquered along the trails, for unable to obtain employment they drifted into one of the too numerous dance-halls, and thence to ruin and disgrace."[9]

But not all the women followed the trade to ruin and disgrace. Although later commentators have tended to conflate the categories, the term *dance*

Dawson City street scene,
1898. *UAF 58-1026-1567 A*

hall girl was never synonymous with *prostitute* in Dawson. Dance hall
workers danced with the miners for a dollar a dance and a percentage of the
liquor they could sell. And many women waltzed the miners on those endless turns around the hall for just a few weeks before moving on to some
other occupation.[10]

In any event, Fannie quickly tired of city life and soon started to follow
the smaller stampedes out of Dawson. The whispered rumor of a strike on
some remote creek was all it took to begin a small rush out of town. Men
and women dropped what they were doing and headed off, usually in the
dead of night to get the jump on other parties. After finding the supposedly
rich creek, prospectors located and staked their claims and then raced back
to Dawson to register them at the recorder's office. Of course, this whole
process was fraught with difficulties. Most of the time, stampeders found
that all the claims were already staked. Sometimes, there would be a problem recording a claim.

It could not have taken Fannie too many of these adventures to realize
that on the longer treks, would-be prospectors who left in a hurry would
often neglect to take adequate provisions with them. So the enterprising
young woman took a sled loaded with provisions—a Yukon stove, along

Fannie in fur jacket, as a young woman in Dawson City. *UAF Fannie Quigley Collection 80-46-210 1898*

with flour, beans, bacon, and coffee—and set up a tent with a sign advertising "Meals for Sale." Cooking and selling food to those who had hiked to the remote creeks was a sure thing, in contrast to the staking itself. In the process, she earned a premium for her cooking skills, as well as a Yukon moniker—"Fannie the Hike."

Undoubtedly the veteran of a number of minor, no-account gold stampedes, Fannie was listed as a "Housekeeper" in Mrs. Ferguson's 1901 city directory. Presumably, Mrs. Ferguson obtained the information for the directory in the preceding summer, so that is probably the job that Fannie left to join the stampede to Clear Creek on the Stewart River in late summer 1900.[11]

CLEAR CREEK

By the late summer of 1900, nearly all the ground in the new Klondike District had been staked, and prospectors began returning to older districts that had been abandoned in the chase for new and greater riches. The Stewart River had been prospected and mined by some of the first prospectors in the Yukon basin (including a young neophyte named Jack London) before the Klondike Stampede.[12] However, like much paying ground in the Yukon, the area had been abandoned when news of the Klondike strikes gave prospectors hope that the pay was better on the other side of the divide. In the fall of 1900, a rush started to the valley of a Stewart River tributary called Clear Creek, so far from the actual Stewart River that the *Klondike Nugget* suggested it should be called something else.

The 125-mile route Fannie took to the new district began by heading up the Klondike River to its headwaters, and then it crossed a swampy divide. As two returning prospectors, Finne and Kagel, described it to the *Klondike Nugget,* "There is a big flat of about twenty-five miles to cross just beyond this divide, and at night, camp fires were seen burning pretty much all over it as far as could be seen."[13] The trip was reported to take eleven days, yet in spite of the area's remote location, the stampede drew large numbers of prospectors. Early returnees who reported in to the papers were suitably enthusiastic and described the country as being similar to that at the famous forks of Eldorado and Bonanza creeks. "On the divide between the Stewart and the Klondike," Finne and Kagel reported, they "met a party of forty from Dominion Creek accompanied by a pack train."

With the discoverer having staked on August 23, 1900, and recorded on August 31, Fannie still arrived in time to stake claim No. 39 Below Discovery on September 17.[14] Ten days later, she was back at the recorder's office in Dawson to file her claim. Frank Slavin, another would-be prospector who returned to Dawson on the same day, reported to the *Klondike Nugget* that his party had gotten lost on the trip into Clear Creek in dense ground fog and rainy weather. By the time they arrived, the creek had been staked all the way up to No. 197 Above.[15]

—⚹—

Nearly one hundred years later, I, too, was consumed with trying to find Clear Creek, a day's expedition from Dawson City. I had persuaded my husband to accompany me on this trip to Dawson with our two small daughters, and we headed out the Klondike Highway, which now follows the valley up the Klondike River. The river itself was dredged long ago, so the natural, clear-running stream slips through a broad stretch of tangled gravel tailings, piles covered now with willows and alders. Leaving town, we crossed the Klondike River and passed Guggieville (a campground for recreational vehicles named for the dredge companies' investors, the Guggenheims) and then the turnoff to the right for the Bonanza Creek Road. Continuing on the highway following the river, we skirted around the base of King Solomon's Dome and crossed Klondike tributaries Bear Creek and then Hunker Creek, which headed back up the dome to our right. Finally, after the Dempster Highway junction took off to the north and the North Fork of the Klondike River split off as well, the route flattened out and the terrain turned featureless. We traversed a low swamp for miles until we reached the turnoff to the Barlow Dome Road, which I had been told led to Clear Creek. The Stewart River itself was some 50 miles down the road.

The Barlow Dome Road, like most in the North, quickly turned to silty, dusty, bumpy, washboarded dirt. Some 5 miles later, heading off seemingly nowhere, the road began to climb and evidence of a great forest fire became apparent in the acres and acres of fire-scarred black spruce. As the road climbed, we looked down a steep slope of scraggly aspens to the valley below. Finally, the road broke into the tundra-covered rocky clearing of the Barlow Dome summit, site of some kind of radar installation. Looking north, we could see in the distance the dramatic snow-capped peaks of the Ogilvie Rockies. And the road kept going. The country seemed suddenly wilder and stranger as we grew woozy with the thickening feeling of not knowing where we were going. With a sense of foreboding, we followed the road as it descended steeply a mile or so into the valley below, and finally we reached the creek, with its piles of overturned gravel indicating mining activity. Crossing on a small homemade bridge, we continued on the right fork, now skirting the base of Barlow Dome, until the road ended less than a mile on at a mining operation, a small cluster of cabins and trailers arrayed among the alder-covered gravel tailings, with a private property sign. Perhaps anticipating the kind of welcome I might get from an Alaskan miner, I could not bring myself to knock on the door, so we absorbed the scenery in the Clear Creek valley and then turned around for the trip back over the dome.

I had studied so many old maps and claims and recorder's logs at the Canadian mining offices that I somehow imagined we would find all the original claim notices and a location notice stating "Fannie was here." I expected to see a clear-running creek in a narrow valley, the remains of a tent fly with a homemade pole table, two stumps for stools, and a Yukon stove. I pictured a young Fannie in a long black skirt and dirty apron cooking pancakes under a rakish, hand-lettered "Meals for Sale" sign.

Of course, in reality, this valley had long ago been mined and mined again and dredged, eventually being grown over in willows and alders. The valley floor has widened and turned to overgrown tailing piles. The site of any turn-of-the-century gold rush had long ago been obliterated. This landscape is all too typical of gold creeks in the North. Originally running in clefts between steep tundra-covered hills and down into wide permafrost valleys, all supporting stands of stunted black spruce, the creeks are different now, their environments changed by the long mining history of the area. Early miners cleared little ground, as they sank shafts for underground mining. But they covered much of the landscape as they pulled the gravel out from the ground and piled it helter-skelter in their ubiquitous dump piles; then they made more of a mess as they altered creek beds to sluice the dumps with the creek water in the spring. Later miners used modern earth-moving equipment to scrape off tundra and topsoil and then moved every cubic foot of gravel as they hauled it to their wash plants and piled up the tailings. Once the original land is disturbed, the unruly alders and willows grow up on the new topography, obscuring all. The alders themselves now mark the sites where the land has been disturbed.

The 1900 rush that lured Fannie to Clear Creek never amounted to much. Though some of the miners did work their claims, most sites were later abandoned. Fannie's claim was canceled like many others for nonrepresentation after she failed to do the assessment work; it was relocated, that is, restaked by some new hopeful soul, in March 1902 and then again in 1903. The 1903 holder kept up the claim by doing the required work annually and then sold out to the famous "Klondike King," Alex McDonald, in 1907. This claim, along with many others, was consolidated in August 1907 to make a large enough block to apply modern, large-scale techniques such as dredging. The sad fact of the mining game was that few of the claims could immediately yield a profit for the staker. Though long-term possibilities might have been promising, it took money to return every year and perform the $100 in assessment work that was required to hold on to the claim, the kind of money that someone such as Fannie never had.

Fannie had been so close to success! Less than 40 miles away, the Duncan Creek area would bring the kind of reward that all prospectors hoped for and that Fannie was to dream about for the rest of her life. Less than three years after she left Clear Creek, prospectors on Duncan Creek, another tributary of the Stewart River, discovered the first galena (silver-lead) ore in the area. Some preliminary mining in the period between 1915 and 1919 brought many more prospectors, leading to the staking of truly rich claims in 1919 and 1920, which were soon leased to major operators, including the Guggenheims. By the fall of 1923, a thousand claims had been staked on Keno Hill. Then in 1925, Charlie Brefelt made a series of discoveries, including the fabulously rich Lucky Strike that assayed at 3,000 ounces of silver per ton and anchored the future development of the district. The galena ore was similar to that developed later by Joe Quigley, Fannie's future husband, in the Kantishna, and ironically, the Treadwell Yukon Company looked at both the Keno Hill properties and Joe's Kantishna properties in 1919. The company settled on developing Keno Hill and became the second-largest producer of silver in Canada and the fourth-largest in the world.[16]

—⁂—

On October 1, 1900, just four days after her return from Clear Creek, Fannie married the dapper Angus McKenzie. Perhaps Angus was also on that rush to Clear Creek. A Canadian from Ottawa, he had arrived in the Yukon in the spring of 1898 before the main rush and had staked a bench claim on French Hill at the junction of French and Eldorado creeks on May 3, 1898. In July, he rushed to Dominion Creek, on the back of King Solomon's Dome, and staked a hillside claim at No. 18 Below Upper Dominion, and in August, he staked another hillside claim on an upper tributary above Bear Creek.[17] He seems to have been almost but not quite in on the good ground

Frances Sedlacek and William Angus McKenzie. *Courtesy of the Oien family*

and managed to stake only the chancier and sometimes worthless bench and hillside claims.

News of the McKenzie marriage was eclipsed by a more prominent union, for October 1, 1900, was also the day that Dawson entrepreneur Belinda Mulrooney, the richest woman in the Klondike, married "Count" Charles Carbonneau, a Quebecois champagne salesman, in a fabulous ceremony at her own Fairview Hotel. The coincidence emphasized the social and monetary distance between wealthy Belinda, at the top of both hierarchies, and Fannie, who was probably closer to the bottom.[18]

After their marriage, Fannie and Angus operated a roadhouse at No. 18 Below on Hunker Creek, about 8 miles up Hunker, past the colorfully named Anderson Concession, Dago Hill, 70 Pup, Lost Chance Creek, and finally the confluence with Gold Bottom Creek. Their new location was not far from another roadhouse at No. 3 Above Hunker Creek where Fannie had already spent some time, according to the story in her obituary.

HUNKER CREEK

By 1901, prospectors had staked claims to nearly every foot of the 18-mile-long Hunker Creek from the head to the flats where it joined the Klondike River. Its many tributaries were rich producers as well, and a well-traveled road ran up the creek, over the dome, and on to Dominion and Sulphur creeks. The town of Gold Bottom sprang up as a major community on the creek, with stores and a Royal Canadian Mounted Police station as well as a hotel. Numerous cabins belonged to miners in the area, many of whom had their families with them. So Fannie's roadhouse was not an isolated spot for travelers but a wayside on a well-used road, not far outside the townsite of Gold Bottom.

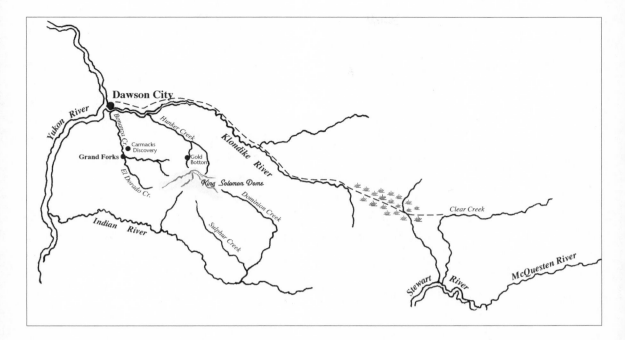

All of this activity was reported in chatty, almost gossipy detail in the *Dawson Daily News Golden Clean-Up Edition,* published on January 1, 1902, in a format designed clearly to boost the potential fortunes of the district. In addition to the ground on Hunker being staked in creek claims to No. 80 Below Discovery, bench claims up the hillsides were staked to the eighth and ninth tier above the creek on the right and left limits. Men "away back up there," as the paper described it, isolated from the main district and far away from the paying ground, were drilling shafts 100 feet deep, hoping to hit another older channel of the creek. Owners of the richer claims could divide them into halves or even smaller fractions and lease them as "lays," which were bought, sold, and traded, won and lost in poker games, or leased again until finally mined by various combinations of individuals and companies. The scene was frenzied mining at all levels of technological development. Some men worked their claims or lays with picks and shovels and primitive rockers or sluice boxes. Others with access to capital imported sophisticated steam pumps and hoists and hired armies of laborers (see Placer Mining in chapter 4).

Fannie was by no means the only woman on the creek. Mrs. Mary Perry owned a fraction on Gold Bottom. Mrs. Curtis, an "enthusiastic amateur photographer," mined with her husband and partners on a hillside claim opposite the upper half of No. 32 Below. The hill on which these bench claims were located was called Temperance Hill—undoubtedly named by a woman (it was probably Mrs. Chambers, owner of the discovery claim on

Fannie's travels in the Klondike. After her initial trip into the Klondike, Fannie traveled extensively, first to Hunker Creek, and then from her home on Hunker Creek east up the Klondike River and over a low swampy pass to a mining strike on Clear Creek, in the Stewart River drainage. *Map by Karen Farrell* the hillside).[19] Nearby, working No. 34 Below, Mrs. Jack Horn had been in the country since 1896, with her husband, an "old-timer." Jack Horn later made the discovery claim on Glacier Creek in the Kantishna with Joe Quigley. Mrs. Horn is never mentioned in Kantishna histories, but perhaps it was through a friendship or acquaintance with the Horns that Fannie found her way to Kantishna.

A roadhouse could be anything from a hovel selling "coffee and sinkers at two bits a throw" to "a substantial two story log hotel with bountiful well cooked meals and substantial cleanly sleeping quarters."[20] An intriguing photo I found years ago in the Yukon Archives in Whitehorse, labeled "#3 Below Hunker Creek," pictures a woman looking very much like Fannie sitting in front of a one-story rough log building. Even if it is not, in fact, Fannie, the structure, the surroundings, and the woman's circumstances would have been very much the same as Fannie's own. Like many such

"I.X.L. Road House #3 Below Hunker Creek." Is this Fannie seated on the steps of this rather primitive roadhouse? Although the name and location do not match any of the roadhouses Fannie was known to have worked at, perhaps the location of the roadhouse where she worked was misstated in other sources, or this roadhouse is misidentified. Or is this just another young woman at a rather primitive roadhouse on Hunker Creek? *Cantwell Photo (1901). YA, Adams & Larkin fonds, #9105*

Staking a Claim

Staking a mining claim was the goal of every one of the thousands making their way to the Klondike. Publishers pounced on the arcane details of Canadian mining law, printing guidebooks and details that were published in newspapers as far away as San Francisco. The subject must have occupied hundreds of hours of discussion on the trip over the passes and down the Yukon River.

The basics were relatively simple. Each prospector had to possess a free miner's certificate, and he or she was able to stake only one claim in any given mining district. A claim ran 500 feet along the creek and from "rim to rim" in the usually narrow valleys. (These laws were modified later to suit conditions.) To stake the claim, one had only to mark the four corners of the area. The usual method was to cut stakes from a nearby tree; identifying information was then written on any handy piece of paper, perhaps the back of a can label. The preferred method of attaching the paper to the stake was to place it in a Prince Albert Tobacco tin that was nailed to the post. George Carmack is said to have identified the discovery claim on Bonanza with a pencil-written note on a tree blaze. The creek claims were given a number and designated as either "Above" or "Below" (that is, either upstream or downstream of the discovery claim).

By the time most of the participants in the great gold rush arrived in the Klondike in the spring of 1898, the thousand or so men and women who had been in the Yukon Basin at the time of the discoveries had already staked most of the claims on the major creeks. Newcomers took their chances on "bench claims," the hillside claims that paralleled the claims in the main creeks. These bench claims were often given colorful names instead of numbers. The old-timers who thought they knew everything about mining made great fun of the "cheechakos," or newcomers, who staked way on up the hillsides, only to be chagrined when one of them discovered the Bonanza's fabulously rich ancient creek bed of eroded quartz, the famed White Channel.

Because only a handful of the newcomers had any idea where or how to find gold, they were uniquely susceptible to stampedes following the latest rumor. The quest was like a game in Dawson, with no real winners. For even if one succeeded in staking a claim, it had to be developed in order to make it pay. Usually, this was an implausible proposition: either there was no gold after all or there was no money to do the development work. If the claim was rich, it would most often be "jumped," that is, staked over by another party, in which case, the courts and expensive litigation were the only recourse. Still, nearly everyone wished to be a player, usually hoping to simply sell out the claim after someone else spent the money developing another claim nearby.

Anna DeGraf, the nearly sixty-year-old seamstress, described one of these adventures:

I did a little staking of my own. . . . The tip was given me by a woman who cooked for the boys at the bank. She sent for me one day and said she had heard there were rich deposits on Hester Creek. She could not leave the bank to go, but said if I would go she would send a man with me to stake for her, and I could stake next to her claim. I said I should try. She warned me that the police boys were all going out to stake there, and that I must get ahead of them.

There were five in our party and we didn't have much of a start on the police boys. We had to walk, and it was bitter cold. After a long tramp we came to a little coffee house and went in to get warm and have a cup of coffee. As we sat at the counter I looked out and saw the police boys coming, five of them. We dropped our cups, slipped out the back door and made a run for it. We took a cut-off and got there first. We had just finished measuring out claims and had our notices posted when the police boys ran up.[21]

Anna and her party hurried back to the coffeehouse, where Anna solicited a ride back to Dawson with a man who had a dog team. "He took me flying to the recorder's Office," she said, "and I was the first to register a claim on Hester Creek, which afterward proved to be rich." Unfortunately for Anna, she failed to do her assessment work, and the claim was jumped, a typical experience.

structures, the roadhouse pictured was built of unpeeled logs and constructed in two 20-foot-long sections. In this summer scene, the roadhouse is surrounded by gravel and mud, like most such structures in the Yukon. In the winter, roadhouses of this type must have been dark, smoky, poorly lit, and crudely furnished.

Fannie and Angus's tenure there as Mr. and Mrs. McKenzie is documented in a December 1901 article in the *Klondike Nugget* reporting on a drunken marital spat. According to the reporter, Fannie and Angus presided over the bar together, occupying a room at the back of the establishment, and they obviously had gotten into a domestic dispute. Angus's plea before the judge, "Drunk but not Intoxicated," apparently amused the reporter for the *Nugget* and induced the paper to print a humorous but jaded summary of the proceeding:

> Angus McKenzie and his wife Fannie conduct a roadhouse on No. 18 Below on Hunker over which until recently the white winged angel of peace was wont to hover while Angus and Fannie, but recently married, would bill and coo beneath their fig tree. At length that demon that biteth like a skeeter and stinketh like a gad fly—hootch, handmade, home brew, pervaded their abode of peace and tranquility and took a lay on Angus, working him almost continuously ever since.[22]

The previous Monday, according to the article, Angus and Fannie had "had a mix-up," and Fannie emerged with an eye "which bears some resemblance to a Boer map." (The reporter was presumably referring to a bloody map of the Anglo-Boer War in South Africa, which was ongoing at the time.) Fannie had Angus arrested for assault and drunk and disorderly conduct. Though admitting he was drunk, Angus told the court that Fannie was drunk as well, "too drunk," according to the paper, "to appear as a bright and shining light in roadhouse company." He claimed "that he had only attempted to induce her to return to her room, and to hasten her retirement, he had gently laid his hands on her to push her along like a good thing; that she had taken offense and had him arrested on the two charges." Together, they paid a thirty-dollar fine and were both released.

Somehow, the couple got through 1902 uneventfully. But it seems doubtful that Angus stopped drinking as he had promised the judge he would. For Fannie, the earlier incident was merely one episode in a lifetime marked by a problem with alcohol, typified by her later association with a home-brewed concoction known as Kantishna champagne.

By the end of 1902, opportunities for the independent miner had waned, as all the major ground in the Klondike had been staked, and stampeders had moved on to Nome. By Christmas, the time was ripe for the rumor that would set off the last of the truly big stampedes, drawing Fannie and thousands of others to the Tanana Valley and the new towns of Fairbanks and Chena.

Walking Out
From the Klondike to Alaska

IT WAS ALWAYS FANNIE'S FORTE to have a jump on the news—to make it to the next strike ahead of the rush. After two tumultuous years of marriage, she left Angus McKenzie and Dawson on January 17, 1903, giving the post-master her new address—Rampart, Alaska. In what was one of the coldest Yukon winters, with temperatures reaching 50° below zero, her 700-mile hike down the Yukon River gave new meaning to the term *walking out:* there was no other means of transportation. On the day she left, the *Yukon Sun* ran the first headline trumpeting the newest find, "Gold in Tanana."[1]

Jujiro Wada, a Japanese miner, cook, and long-distance runner, had arrived in Dawson with two companions from somewhere west of the Alaskan border with the story of the next big "Klondike in America." Short on news, the paper pumped the story with a picture of Wada, a crude map, and Wada's version of the gold strike. In all probability, Wada had been sent to Dawson to hype the new district by his employer, trader E. T. Barnette. According to the *Yukon Sun,* Wada had left the banks of the Chena River on December 28, during the coldest and darkest part of the winter. When he arrived in Dawson, he reported that news of the strike had already spread to Circle, Eagle, and Rampart and that the thirty men from Rampart had arrived in the new camp just the evening before he departed.[2]

But as had happened in earlier stampedes, most of the residents of Dawson would cautiously wait for news from a trusted source before heading out themselves. If Fannie had friends in Rampart, it was likely she had heard of the strike from them. Rampart itself had been the scene of a gold strike in the same year as the Klondike, and many of the men who had rich claims

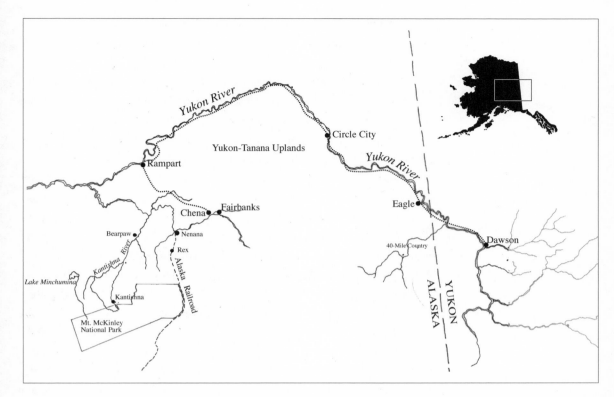

there had stayed. The little town on the Yukon was only 60 miles or so overland from the newly discovered creeks in the Tanana, and men from Rampart had, in fact, started their own stampede a month before while the news of the strike was just reaching Dawson. Rampart men were among the first in the new camp and instrumental in the founding of Chena, one of the two new towns in the district.[3]

After Fannie was well on her way, in early 1903, the story of the new strike hit Dawson with a vengeance, and another stampede was on. By February, hundreds of stampeders were leaving Dawson, and reports of their departures and other information and speculation from and about the new camp began to appear in the *Klondike Nugget* almost daily. According to the March 4 report, "In the month of February, two hundred stampeders left Dawson for the lower country." Another letter received in Dawson reported there were 150 men on the trail from Rampart to the Tanana.[4]

The prospect of a fresh opportunity was especially popular among those who had failed in Dawson and gone into debt, for they were able to cross the border and escape their debts while the authorities were off duty. The *Daily Klondike Nugget* noted on March 4 that "Saturday Night has been the most favored time for the departure of such gentry as with a good team of dogs the run to the boundary line can be made before Monday morning."

Fannie's travels down the Yukon. As she left Dawson, Fannie walked down the Yukon River to Rampart, then on to Chena and Fairbanks. *Map by Karen Farrell*

The previous Saturday night, the *Nugget* continued, "between the hours of 11 o'clock and 2 in the morning no less that twenty-two persons got away under the cover of darkness."[5]

The Dawson Fannie was leaving was hardly in decline. But many independent miners who had been attracted by the promise of the frontier, the opportunities for independence, the chance at the big strike, and the wide-open town realized that their game was up in Dawson. The great Klondike gold rush that captured the imagination of the world was really a prelude to the large-scale, capital-intensive, corporate mining that was to follow and last for another sixty years. Where the *Dawson Daily News Golden Clean-Up Edition* of New Year's Day 1902 had highlighted the work of hundreds of independent miners, the news just one year later was focused on the large placer concessions, spearheaded by Arthur Treadgold and Joe Boyle.[6] Three years previously, the White Pass and Yukon Railway had finished a line from Skagway to Whitehorse, and large, well-equipped, and elaborately fitted steamboats completed the trip to Dawson City. Now, the gold rush of 1898, with its two- or three-month journey over the Chilkoot Pass and down treacherous river rapids and all the attendant hardships, was becoming a pioneer memory as Dawson settled into a more stable middle age.

Once the transportation links had been established, many more women arrived in the area, and they brought a new social order that emphasized middle-class respectability to what had seemed to some a nearly classless society. Many of the early prospectors and most of the "sporting element"— the gamblers and saloon owners—had left the Klondike to join the rush to Nome in 1899 after the discoveries on the Seward Peninsula in 1898. Where once women had been an unusual sight, where the dance hall girls and prostitutes were the favorites of the town, now the miners thought more of their wives and mothers. Women had established a social pecking order, not only in Dawson but on the creeks as well. The *Klondike Nugget* now had a regular social feature chronicling the women's Thursday afternoons receiving at home and their whist parties and other social affairs. The social gulf was only widening between the newly arrived middle-class Canadian and American women—nurses, teachers, and wives of upstanding miners and businessmen—and the women of humbler origins. And for Fannie, the immigrant wife of a bartending former prospector with a drinking problem, it was clearly time to move on.[7]

—∞—

The town of Forty Mile was a good day's run from Dawson by Ben Downing's stage line or by a fast dog team. The boundary itself was about 90 miles downstream from Dawson, and at least those dishonest debtors who did not stop at Forty Mile were able to make it over the border in a day and a half. Just across the border, which had finally been fixed in 1887, Fannie would have come to Eagle City. In 1898, it had been hardly a village, but by 1903, it was the site of the U.S. Army's Fort Egbert, the court established by Judge James Wickersham, and American customs. Eagle was the jumping-off and supply point for local mining activity. More important, it was the site of the headquarters of Lt. Billy Mitchell and his team, who were engaged in building the new telegraph line—the Washington-Alaska Military Cable/System and Telegraphy, known as WAMCATS. As the rush grew, many Tanana stampeders attempted to travel along Mitchell's telegraph route to the new goldfields.

Fannie developed her literacy and the ability to write letters only after some years in the North: she left no diaries or memoir. But even though she did not herself document the times she knew and the places she traveled, her trails in the North were destined to follow those of Judge Wickersham. Wickersham, a Republican lawyer from Tacoma, Washington, who had garnered an appointment as the first U.S. district court judge in the interior of Alaska, had arrived in Eagle with his wife and young son in 1900. It is thanks to Wickersham's extensive diaries and memoir that we have a vivid picture of this portion of Fannie's journey.[8]

As the only judge in all of the interior, Wickersham headed down the Yukon River from Eagle by dog sled in the winter of 1901 to hold a term of court in Rampart in order to settle some claim-jumping cases. Fannie's trip from Eagle to Rampart two years later closely followed the judge's route. Of course, Wickersham could afford to hire the best dog team and driver-guide, and he was well provisioned for the trip. By contrast, Fannie probably walked, perhaps accompanied by a few dogs. Wickersham's total expenses for his dog team, driver, roadhouse expenses, meals, and beds amounted to $705. A hardy outdoorsman, he reported that he thoroughly enjoyed the trip, even though he walked most of the way ahead of the team in temperatures ranging from 20 to 50° below zero.

Leaving Eagle, Wickersham wrote, "The great river is walled in by mountain heights forested with spruce. Between Eagle and Circle City there were no towns or permanent settlements, but here and there on the bank of the river was a roadhouse, or a mail-carrier's or a wood-chopper's cabin."[9] Wickersham's 520-mile trip from Eagle to Rampart took twenty-two days. He began on February 9 and arrived in Rampart on March 2, covering an average of more than 23 miles per day. From Eagle, the trail followed another 100 miles or more of twisting river bends beneath high bluffs to Circle

City. Once touted as "the Paris of the North," Circle City had been established after a gold strike on nearby Birch Creek in 1893 and originally boasted 1,500 lively inhabitants. But the town had emptied out in the spring of 1897 as nearly every inhabitant left for the Klondike. Circle in 1903 still supported a small mining community, and it was now a trailhead for a new trail through the Birch Creek diggings and over Twelve Mile Summit and Eagle Summit to the new Tanana Mining District. By late spring, most stampeders to the Tanana would use the Circle Trail, a 240-mile route to the Tanana. However, early on, little news had filtered back to Dawson regarding the best routes, and so, for Fannie, continuing on down the Yukon to Rampart and a known route would have been a safer choice.

Even as early as 1900, the Yukon River Trail, like nearly all the well-traveled trails in the North, was punctuated by a series of roadhouses about 15 miles apart. Wickersham named nearly every roadhouse and cabin that he passed along the way, though he did not stop at all of them. He mentioned the Star Roadhouse, the Montauk Roadhouse, the Nation River Roadhouse, the Coal Creek Roadhouse, Webber's Roadhouse, and Johnson's Roadhouse, just 22 miles from Circle. He stopped at the Charley River Indian Roadhouse and then went 45 miles farther to the Half-Way Roadhouse. Next came Seventeen-Mile Cabin, Fort Yukon, and, 34 miles beyond that, Britt's Cabin. Victor's Cabin and Smith's came next, followed by Wood-Chopper Carsh's, Ross' Cabin, Tucker's Cabin, and finally Rampart.

Most of these establishments were nothing more than the roughest sort of cabins, many belonging to men who were engaged in cutting the vast quantities of wood needed to fuel the huge steamboats that plied the river in the summer. But at them, the mail carrier and other assorted travelers could find shelter, a woodstove, and a place for their dogs. Wickersham colorfully described the typical fare at Webber's Roadhouse:

> The fame of the landlord's rabbit stew had spread along the trail. The stew was prepared in a large kerosene can on top of an ancient Yukon sheet-iron stove set on the dirt floor and held in place by a low, rough frame of logs. In this can the famed rabbit stew always simmered. As hungry guests at the pole table reduced its contents, more water, rabbit, caribou, bear, or lynx was added. From early in November when the first ice permitted travel on the great river highways . . . until the following May, break-up, the odor and steam from this ragout of wild meats permeated the tavern. . . . But we ate it and paid two dollars each per meal for it.[10]

Did Fannie herself crowd into these roadhouses among the men? Many women did (they often mentioned that a bunk or end of the room was curtained off for their use). Somehow, I imagine Fannie would have avoided these places. I think of her as too independent, too accustomed to camping out and fending for herself, and I suspect she would have been wary of exposing herself as a woman traveling alone.

At Circle, the Yukon River broke out of the rolling hill country and entered the maze of the Yukon Flats—hundreds of square miles of swamps and sloughs. At the top of the northern arc of the Yukon River, the Porcupine River joined in, flowing down from the far north. There, in the heart of the Yukon Flats, 50 miles downriver from Circle, travelers arrived at the missionary and trading village of Fort Yukon. From Fort Yukon, the trail followed the great river highway as it swept to the southwest. Finally, just where the river choked up again and entered the hills was the narrow walled canyon called the Ramparts of the Yukon and the town of Rampart, Fannie's immediate destination.

Rampart, Alaska, was one of the thriving mining communities on the Yukon River, a kind of a halfway point between Dawson and Nome. John Minook had discovered gold in Little and Big Minook creeks there in 1897, and trader Al Mayo and his family built the new Alaska Commercial Company store.[11] Some observers reported that Minook's strike alone would have been enough to cause a stampede from the States if it had not been eclipsed by the Klondike discoveries the same year. Rampart had become an important way station for Klondike stampeders. The population had reached fifteen hundred over the 1898–99 winter when hundreds of stampeders became stranded on their way to the Klondike. Among the residents that winter were Wyatt Earp and his wife, Josephine, who were stranded on their way to Dawson. They in turn occupied a cabin that had just been abandoned by Rex Beach, who would one day write a novel based on his adventures there.[12] Also in residence that winter were playwright Wilson Mizner; Tex Rickard, later the impresario of Madison Square Garden; and Erastus Brainerd, whose gold rush propaganda for the Seattle Chamber of Commerce was so convincing that he joined the rush himself.

After 1900, many of Mrs. Margaret Mayo's Koyukon Athabascan kin had also settled in the town, now the center of a thriving mining district, making it one of the earliest truly mixed-race communities on the river. Residents and business owners from Rampart were among the first to rush to the Tanana Valley following the initial discoveries of gold in 1902.

The new find in the Tanana Valley was not altogether surprising: in fact, many had expected it. The search for gold in Alaska and the Yukon

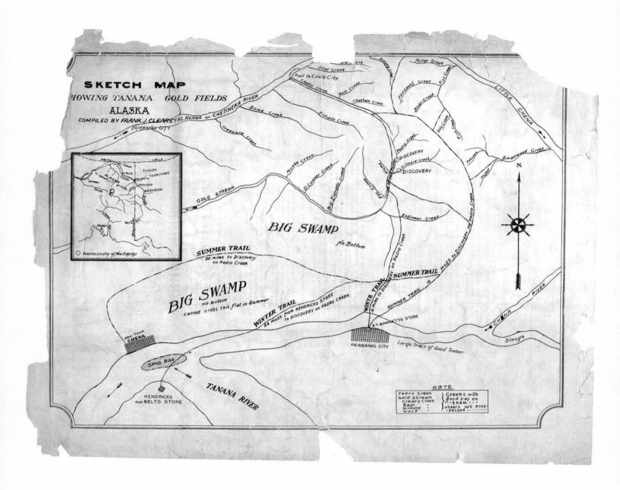

Sketch map of the Tanana Valley goldfields, showing Fairbanks, Chena, the major creeks, and the trails. Drawn by Frank J. Cleary in 1904. *Published in "The Tanana Gold Fields" (Fairbanks, AK: Mason & Hill, May 1904). UAF*

intensified after the Klondike strike, with thousands of men and women arriving in the North to pursue it. Since the gold in the Circle and Fortymile districts was found in streams flowing into the Yukon River from the north side of the Tanana Hills, it seemed likely to many that the south side of the hills had to contain gold as well. But this area was even more remote and difficult to access because it was far from the Yukon River, the main highway of the North. Even amid the vast wilderness areas of Alaska, the land lying between the Yukon and Tanana rivers, called the Yukon-Tanana uplands, was a largely inaccessible quarter. The old, worn-down, rocky terrain and the intensely dry climate of the interior added up to a tangle of high, steep, rocky-topped hills, cut through with the narrow valleys of just a few small twisting and turning streams.

(Flying over the area a few years ago in a light plane, I nearly lost my stomach: the high hills cause violent updrafts and ominous thunderheads. Bumping over the hilltops, it seemed the plane would not even clear the highest of them, with their scaly exposed summits. As I imagined a forced landing, my eyes fruitlessly tried to trace a trail out, any trail. It is still the forgotten quarter, a place to get lost. If we did crash, I thought, how would they ever find us? All the hills and valleys looked the same.)

Nevertheless, a few determined prospectors had been exploring the hundreds of creek valleys since the early days. The most determined of these men was Italian immigrant Felice Pedroni, who went by the anglicized name Felix Pedro. On an 1898 trip down the Tanana, Pedro had discovered a rich creek, but then, short of supplies, he had been forced to leave the site. He spent the next four years searching the look-alike hills and valleys for his original claim, said to be somewhere near the headwaters of the Goodpasture or Salcha rivers, tributaries of the Tanana draining the uplands. In the late spring of 1901, he had enough resources to put together an outfit and return to the area with his partner, Tom Gilmore. Leaving Eagle Creek, in the Birch Creek District, they followed the high ridges between the Chena and the Chatanika, sampling some of the creeks on the way. Crossing into the Goldstream Valley, they headed down valley hoping to reach the Tanana.[13]

Converging on the same area was the U.S. Army Signal Corps telegraph crew, constructing a telegraph line that would link Dawson, Eagle, Tanana, and Valdez. The Signal Corps built a station at the mouth of the Chena in 1900. Meanwhile, traders Nathan Hendricks and George Belt, from Rampart, had established a new post across the Tanana from the mouth of the Chena River in 1901 to serve the Signal Corps. Belt and Hendricks, who had already been operating on the Tanana for a few years, had picked their site carefully, as they knew it was the head of navigation on the Tanana, as far as a river steamer could proceed before reaching the formidably shallow water called Bates Rapids.

Then, in midsummer 1901, trader E. T. Barnette, together with his wife, Isabelle, and a party of others, chartered the small steamer *Lavelle Young* under Captain Charles Adams in St. Michael. They headed up the Tanana, hoping to set up a trading post on the upper Tanana River. Jujiro Wada was in the Barnette party, serving as the cook. Adams, like every other northern river man, knew that Barnette would get no farther than the rapids, but the trader was determined. So Adams made a deal with him: he would take Barnette as far up the river as they could get, and then Barnette would have to unload his goods. (It is difficult and dangerous to take a fully loaded steamboat downstream.) Heading up the Tanana past the mouth of the Chena Slough, the *Lavelle Young* hit bottom at Bates Rapids, as predicted. Captain Adams made one attempt to go around via the Chena, which supposedly connected back with the main river. But again, the riverboat went aground when it hit a sandbar. Isabelle Barnette endured the waning days of fall listening to the captain and her husband argue about the steamer's progress, as the willows and alders lining the banks of the river turned red and yellow and the nights grew steadily colder. Finally, the captain unloaded the Barnettes, their party, and their goods on the high, spruce-covered bank of the Chena River, about 8 miles up the slough from Hendricks and Belt's post on the Tanana, but with no prospective trading partners in sight.

As Barnette and Adams argued in August 1901, Pedro and Gilmore were climbing to the top of the highest hill in the area (now called Pedro Dome) when they sighted the steamer's smoke from the summit.[14] Barnette and his crew were cutting the spruce to build a small stockade when the two prospectors appeared out of the woods, hoping to get supplies. It was a lucky stroke of fate for Barnette, who now had at least the hope that there might be a gold strike nearby. Over the next months, E. T. and Isabelle traded the remainder of their goods with the local Athabascan bands for furs, and then they left the post in midwinter, mushing over the Alaska Range to Valdez and heading for San Francisco, where they spent the remainder of the winter in the Palace Hotel. They left Isabelle's brother, Frank Cleary, in charge of the trading post.

Pedro and Gilmore had continued on to the upper Salcha River, where they thought they found the rich creek that Pedro had explored a few years earlier; they named it '98 Creek, inspiring a minor stampede from Circle in late summer 1901. But the stampede went bust when the claims proved to have little value. Gilmore eventually returned to Circle, too, and Pedro went back alone in 1902 to dig test shafts into the creeks they had passed over in 1901. He returned to Barnette's new post for more supplies, and against the express instructions of Barnette, Cleary grubstaked him. When the Barnettes returned, it was to news that, miraculously, in July 1902, Pedro had found gold. While the five or six men at the post staked claims in the area immediately, word spread quickly back to Pedro's associates in Circle. Soon, more than twenty of them made their way to the new district and staked claims on the newly discovered creeks as well, and Pedro went on to stake discovery claims on Gilmore and Goldstream creeks. The prospectors arriving from Circle concentrated their claims on the creeks north of town, but the prospectors from Rampart, arriving from the west, explored and staked claims in the district surrounding Ester Dome, closer to their base at Chena. Then, just before Christmas 1902, Barnette sent Jujiro Wada to Dawson to spread the news of the new district. While men and women from Rampart trickled into the new camp through January and February, hundreds began to leave Dawson.

In March, George Belt left his trading post on the Tanana and traveled to Dawson to attract his own stampeders. Hendricks and Belt moved their post across the Tanana River to a site at the base of Chena Ridge.[15] The new settlement of Chena was platted, with stampeders from Rampart staking most of the lots. When he arrived in Dawson after a trip of only eleven days, Belt reported that there were five hundred men in the camp already (he did not say how many women), and one hundred buildings were being erected in Chena, including one saloon started by a Circle man.

The settlements at Chena and Barnette's Cache became rivals for the trade to the new district. Chena was certainly more accessible for the steamboat traffic on the Tanana River, but Barnette's Cache was closer to the newly discovered creeks radiating from Pedro Dome, and it was favored by Pedro and the crowd from Circle. Moreover, political clout was on the side of Barnette's post. At the suggestion of Judge Wickersham, Barnette had named his townsite Fairbanks after the powerful Republican U.S. senator, Charles W. Fairbanks. That Wickersham would favor Fairbanks with the courthouse and jail on his arrival in the spring of 1903 was nearly inevitable.

Chena, view by L. E. Robertson, 1905. Chena, founded by miners from Rampart, was a competing townsite to Fairbanks. *UAF Erskine Collection 1970-0028-0101*

There is very little information about what Fannie actually did during her three years in the Fairbanks area. Her assertion that she was heading for Rampart is really all we have to go on, so we have to assume that she settled in Chena, along with most of the Rampart stampeders and because Chena was out of the mainstream. Although Fannie was probably one of the first in the new district, it was not until March 1904 that she staked her initial claim on Alder Creek, a tributary of Cripple Creek, about 15 miles west of Fairbanks near the present town of Ester. The area eventually proved to be one of the richest in the district—but only after Fannie had sold her claim.[16]

Barnette's greed and the greed of others ended up backfiring. The miners who arrived from Rampart and Dawson in the early months of 1903 found that the ground was staked and only limited work was going on. Barnette had staked ten claims for himself and twenty-five for friends and relatives through powers of attorney. The idea was to let someone else develop an adjacent claim, proving the richness of the creek, and then sell out. But the power-of-attorney claims strangled the district, since few of them were being worked. With very little gold to show for it their efforts, men who had left paying claims in Rampart returned to work them. But those who arrived later from Dawson were 800 miles farther from home. Consequently, the stampede, which had burned so brightly, was virtually over by breakup, the season of mud when the snow melts in early May. The only money in the camp was what the stampeders had brought with them, and food was scarce. A mob of resentful miners suspected Barnette of hoarding and threatened to storm the trader's post, as well as lynch Wada, the messanger who was sent to Dawson. Barnette defended the post with armed guards. Nonetheless, a cursory sort of impoverished log cabin town materialized while everyone waited for the gold to come out of the ground and the good times to begin. Meanwhile, the serious prospectors struck out for creeks farther afield.

Unlike in the Klondike, where gold in the streams was close to the surface and miners washing out their pay dirt in gold pans found as much as $300 per pan the first winter, the gold in Fairbanks was deep underground; the ancient streambeds on the bedrock had been covered by even more eroded dirt from the hillsides. But the newly arrived prospectors on the creeks in the Tanana District were not novices. Veterans of many gold rushes large and small in the Yukon Basin, from Fortymile and Birch Creek to the Klondike and Minook Creek, they were prepared to stay and dig in, using 15-, 50-, and even 200-foot shafts if they had to. The five years since the Klondike gold rush had seen phenomenal improvements in technology. The miners knew that once they had access to steam boilers with steam points that could drive the steam deep into the permafrost, as well as steam to power the windlasses to bring out the dirt from the shafts, the ground would pay off. Of course, all of this took money—capital investment. With a 200-hundred foot shaft needed, at the cost of $10 a foot, this was no get-rich-quick gold rush for the tenderfoot, or cheechako. That is why mining was disappointing during the summer of 1903, with little gold actually recovered though many more creeks were staked. The Rampart papers complained that the whole rush was a hoax.

Ironically, by the fall of 1903, due to reports about a bust, there were few supplies in the area. The enterprising Barnette, taking advantage of the early hopes for the district, had sold out to the Northern Commercial Company, and now the company warned of a shortage of food. The few miners who remained managed to eke out a subsistence livelihood over the winter. But by the spring of 1904, things were turning around. Their efforts were finally paying off, and the boats from Dawson City brought many more miners from Dawson, along with the shopkeepers and businesspeople who hoped to profit from a new gold rush. Now when the miners ventured into the growing town of Fairbanks, they recognized the same signs on the same businesses they had left in Dawson, with familiar faces inside. That fall, when the newspaper published its "Tanana Goldfields Edition," Fairbanks had 1,200 inhabitants and over 500 houses, making it the largest log cabin town in the North. In addition, there were 1,500 to 1,800 more people on the creeks, as the work of sinking shafts continued.[17]

By the time Fannie left Dawson City in 1903, her sisters Josephine and Mary, both married, had emigrated to the West Coast—Josephine to Oregon and Mary to Washington. If Fannie had the resources to travel to the Tanana, at least a month's trip overland on foot or by dog team, she must also have had the resources for a trip to Seattle. Nevertheless, she chose not to go back. Instead, like many others, she opted to follow the frontier into the interior of Alaska, to pursue the elusive dream of the prospector to get in on the next big strike—to get to the scene of the excitement, outsmart all of the other stampeders, and hopefully make her stake.

As mentioned, Fannie spent nearly three years in the Fairbanks area. When she arrived, she had been in the North for almost five years and was an old hand at mining claims, camp cooking, and roadhouse operation. She would have found ready use for all those talents either in Fairbanks or in one of the many small settlements on the creeks. But although city directories listed persons in all of the settlements, her name has not come to light in any such roster, nor did it appear in the local newspaper. Thus, what she actually did between spring 1903 and fall 1905 remains a mystery.

By 1905, Chena had lost out to Fairbanks as the district center, and the early days of rushing and staking were over. With the gold lying deep underground, the claims in production were turning to a corporate mining model, with extensive capitalization and hired labor. The entire district was mired in litigation over the original power-of-attorney claims. It was no longer a place for the independent miner to make a stake. All of Fairbanks was listening for the whisper of the next big thing, eager for a rush to the next new discovery.

Surprisingly enough, the whisper came via Judge Wickersham himself. In the early spring of 1903, he had been seized with the desire to climb Mount McKinley, the massive mountain visible on Fairbanks's southern horizon. Wickersham made inquiries among the local Dené, as the Wood River and Chena Athabascans called themselves, and they pointed him toward the Kantishna River as the route to the mountain. As they proceeded along that route, Wickersham and his companions sampled the creeks for gold, and on their return, they filed claims in Rampart. Joe Quigley was among the prospectors who took up the challenge and spent most of 1904 and 1905 exploring the Kantishna Hills, finally relocating to his new discoveries. Some reports suggest that Fannie met Joe while she worked as a nurse and he was ill with typhoid in Fairbanks in 1903. This story suggests that Fannie moved to Kantishna to be with Joe. Many other versions claim that they were already married when they settled there as a couple. The truth is somewhat more complicated.

Into Kantishna

MOUNT MCKINLEY

Fannie McKenzie had left her husband in the Klondike and followed the trail of Judge James Wickersham down the Yukon River. Both stampeded to the new gold rush in the Tanana in 1903, and Wickersham's explorations were to play yet another major role in Fannie's destiny, when he decided to climb Mount McKinley. The claims staked by his climbing party and recorded in Rampart would soon lead prospectors, among them Joe Quigley and Fannie herself, to the Kantishna area.

Wickersham first sighted Mount McKinley from the top of Cleary Summit on his trip by dog team into the Tanana Valley in the spring of 1903. The Tanana is a major tributary of the Yukon, and although its waters run some 800 miles to the Bering Sea, the valley floor, a tree-covered carpet bisected by the gleaming braided strands of the river, is at an elevation of only 400 feet. To the southeast, the chiseled, snow-capped peaks of the Alaska Range, 250 miles distant and rising some 12,000 to 13,000 feet, appear over the horizon. Mount McKinley, 180 miles away, appears as a ghostly massif anchoring the west end of the Alaska Range as it makes a turn to the south.

At 20,320 feet, Mount McKinley is the tallest mountain in North America, and with its enormous bulk rising above 200 miles of valley floor, it has one of the greatest vertical rises of any mountain in the world. The clear, crisp spring air in the interior brings it into focus, making it seem much closer than it is. Wickersham wrote in his diary that spring of 1903:

The oftener one gazes upon its stupendous mass, the stronger becomes the inclination to visit its base and spy out the surroundings. From the moment we reached the Tanana Valley, the longing to approach it had been in my mind; now the opportunity was at hand. Could we blaze a trail into a distant and unknown wilderness of forest and mountain, extend geographic knowledge and possibly aid in the development of a new mining camp? After much cogitation, I began to organize a party for the trip.[1]

Although many explorers imagined the area to be a vast and untouched wilderness, this was not strictly true in any sense. Lower Tanana and Koyukon Athabascan bands inhabited the whole drainage of the Tanana River, with camps and villages at Wood River, Toltchaket, Togethelle, Minto, Tolovana, and down to the great trading site of Nuklukayet at the junction of the Tanana and Yukon rivers. They lived and hunted on the Kantishna, the lower Toklat, and in the Lake Minchumina region and carried on trade with groups to the south, over well-traveled trails. The Kantishna River drainage was a part of this trade network, a great green swath of nearly flat lowlands north and west of the forbidding Alaska Range, connecting the Tanana Valley with the headwaters of the Kuskokwim, the major river of southwest Alaska.

Wickersham was singularly well prepared for his explorations. He had dabbled in ethnology in the Puget Sound area and had more respect for the Native Alaskans than the average white explorer. He began consulting a band of Natives from the Kantishna River area who were then camped near Chena. They described the river, which they told him flowed from the slopes of the "great mountain." In addition, a different class of adventurer had already discovered the region. Numerous traders, trappers, and prospectors had traveled in the area since the late 1880s, lured by tales of gold in the Yukon basin. Men such as Henry Davis had traveled from Fortymile down the Yukon and then spread out, moving across the country; they prospected, when possible, and trapped, traded, hunted, and built cabins to sustain themselves. As early as 1888 and 1889, Davis and other prospectors had traveled, hunted, trapped, and prospected in the lower Yukon, at Fort Yukon, in the Tanana, and at the mouth of the Kantishna. They explored the Kantishna River and crossed over the portage to the Kuskokwim via Lake Minchumina.[2] When geologist Alfred Brooks led an expedition to the area for the U.S. Geological Survey in 1902, he noted the difference between the trappers and the professional explorers. "Often these pioneers make journeys that would put to shame the widely advertised explorations

of many a well-equipped government expedition," he said. "Were the results of their efforts commensurate with the toil, danger, and suffering involved, geographical sciences would be much enriched thereby. Unfortunately, their ideas of where they have been are almost as vague as of where they are going."[3]

The Brooks expedition started at tidewater on Cook Inlet. The large party of men and pack animals toiled through the valley of the Yentna River in the wet, swampy country on the south side of the Alaska Range. With only vague directions, they crossed the range at Rainy Pass, now known as a part of the Iditarod Trail. Then they turned northeast and traversed the dry plain north of the range to the base of Mount McKinley, where Brooks himself took part of a day to ascend the moraine of Peters Glacier. They continued through the high passes that are now the route of

Judge James Wickersham *(right)* with a Tolovana Chief *(left)* and one of the chief's friends. Wickersham's attempt to climb Mount McKinley brought attention to the Kantishna as a potential mining district. *ASL PCA 277-11-57* the Park Road and on to Nenana. In a 1902 *National Geographic* article, Brooks suggested the Peters Glacier as a route for climbing the mountain.

Judge Wickersham might have seemed an unlikely figure to organize and carry out what would be one of the truly remarkable trips in the annals of Alaska exploration. He was, after all, forty-six in the spring of 1903, and his portly physique did not suggest an outdoorsman. But as it happened, he did have perhaps the perfect portfolio of experience to carry out his plan. From his years as an attorney in Tacoma, Washington, he was familiar with Mount Rainier, which rises to over 14,000 feet southeast of that city. He had advocated for a change of name for the peak, back to the Indian name of Tacoma. He had also hiked extensively in the Cascades and on the Olympic Peninsula. Whether or not he himself had actually climbed Rainier, it seems likely that he had was at least familiar with the mountaineer's sport. He was also widely read and undoubtedly familiar with the Brooks article published in *National Geographic*. In his years in Tacoma, Wickersham had also visited with the local Indians, interviewed them, and written a number of ethnological reports. Respectful of Indian knowledge, Wickersham visited with some of the local bands camped near Fairbanks and asked for their geographic advice, which led to his success in finding the Kantishna River as the key to reaching the base of the mountain.

The *Tanana Chief* at the mouth of the Kantishna River. This is the small steamboat that took Wickersham and friends some ways up the Kantishna to begin their climb of Mount McKinley. *UAF Charles Sheldon Collection*

With his secretary, George Jeffrey, Wickersham had already traveled extensively through the interior, in winter and summer, in the course of performing his court duties. To complete his party, Wickersham chose Mort Stevens, "six feet tall and an all around athlete"; Charlie Webb, "packer and woodsman"; and John McLeod, son of a Hudson Bay Company trader who spoke most of the Tena (Dene) dialects, who would serve as an interpreter.[4]

The party left Chena on May 16, 1903. They headed down the Tanana River on a small river steamer, the *Tanana Chief*, to the mouth of the Kantishna River and then persuaded Captain Hendricks to take them partway up. "The Kantishna is as large as the Wabash, the Sacramento, or the Illinois," enthused Wickersham about the wide lower river. Fifteen miles upstream, they came to the camp of Nacherea and fifty members of his band. McLeod translated for Wickersham, who wanted to tell the Athabascans of his wish to reach the summit of the big mountain: "Incredulity appeared on every face at the statement of our purpose: 'We go merely to see the top, to be the first to reach the summit.' This information . . . caused [the leader] Olyman to remark in brief Indian phrases, which McLeod translated after the rude laughter had subsided as: 'He says you are a fool.'"[5]

Nevertheless, using charcoal on birch bark, the old hunters drew them a map "showing the rivers falling away from the high one, and giving us distances from point to point in that direction." The party divided in two, with Jeffrey and McLeod traveling overland with the party's two mules

The Kantishna River winds through the Tanana flats in this early aerial view. *UAF Charles Sheldon Collection* (named Mark and Hannah after President William McKinley's famous political mastermind, who was the judge's nemesis). Wickersham, Webb, and Stevens took the supplies in the small boat they had found at the mouth of the river and named the *Mudlark*. For the remainder of the trip in the shallow stream, they would be poling upriver, in the traditional fashion of voyageurs and prospectors, with one man in the rear of the boat pushing with a long pole and the others on shore pulling with a long rope. Still, they were not yet "off the beaten trail," beyond the range of white prospectors and traders. They encountered three trappers, including two who had been on the Kuskokwim and were traveling back via Lake Minchumina to sell their furs. These men drew yet another map for Wickersham's party. And they visited Native camps and consulted with the hunters on the river at Tuktawgana, the spring and summer camp of Koonah's band, and at the mouth of the Chitsiana, the camp of Anotoktilon, head of a band of Athabascans from Lake Minchumina.

On June 3, they staked the first gold claims in the area after finding some "colors," or fine flakes of gold, on Chitsia Creek. Discovery Claim was staked for Wickersham opposite the mouth of Two Moose Gulch. Then the climbing expedition continued. On June 13, they reached the valley of the McKinley Fork and the base of the mountain. Following Brooks's map, they headed toward the Peters Glacier and made their final camp at 5,000 feet.

The weather had been hot and sunny, so the party took to traveling at night when the glacier ice and snow was at its most firm. At 10 p.m. on June 20, the summer solstice, the longest day of the year, Wickersham left camp with Webb, Jeffrey, and Stevens for what they expected to be their final attempt to ascend Mount McKinley, each with a knapsack, 100 feet of rope, and an alpenstock. They hiked for nine hours on the wide glacier as the sun hugged the north horizon, dipped briefly below it, and then rose again. At seven the next morning, they reached a point of rocks overlooking the glacier where they could finally see that their "high road to the summit" terminated in an impassable 10,000-foot wall of ice and granite. Now known as the Wickersham Wall, this north face is one of the most formidable vertical faces in mountaineering lore. The warm weather was against them: the midsummer sun unleashed numerous snowslides and avalanches. "These beautiful, cloudless summer days have made the monster mountain sweat," wrote Wickersham. "We recognize we are inviting destruction by staying here and have reluctantly concluded there is no possible chance of further ascent from this side of Denali at this season, or any other for that matter." Satisfied that they had made their best effort, they descended for the return trip to Rampart, where Wickersham was due to preside over a new term of the court.[6]

For the return trip, they built a raft, and two of the men boarded it to float down the McKinley Fork to the Kantishna, while the others led the mules through the underbrush. Almost immediately, the raft was caught in unforeseen rapids. Luckily, the two men survived, but the accident cost them most of their remaining supplies. For more than a week, they subsisted on plain moose meat cooked on sticks directly over the fire, with no salt. They finally reached the Tanana River on July 5 and continued on to the Yukon, where they waited for a river steamboat to take them upriver to Rampart.

The pioneering expedition had not succeeded in conquering the mountain, but the men did record the Chitsia Creek claims together with a rough map of the vicinity, thereby opening a vast new country for prospecting and exploration. Wickersham also published an article in *National Geographic*, further fueling interest and speculation among eastern scientists and explorers in conquering the mountain. As a miner, Fannie would be one of those who benefited from Wickersham's pioneering explorations, and for the rest of her days in the Kantishna, her life would intersect with scientists and explorers who were drawn, like Wickersham, to Mount McKinley. Once again, Wickersham's well-documented trip revealed just how remote the Kantishna District was even from Fairbanks and how difficult it was to travel there, only two years before Fannie moved there herself.

KANTISHNA GOLD

Wickersham's claims drew prospectors' attention to the Kantishna area in the summer of 1903. From Fairbanks or Rampart, as one approaches from the north via the Tanana River, the peaks and domes of the high hills gradually become visible in a curving arc from Chitsia in the northeast to Kankone Peak, Glacier Peak, Wickersham Dome, and Busia Mountain and Brooker Mountain at the southwest end, closest to Mount McKinley. If they were located in Vermont or North Carolina, these "hills" would be called mountains, akin to the Adirondacks or the Green Mountains. (The tallest mountain in Vermont, Mount Mansfield, is 4,393 feet high.) But here in the shadow of Mount McKinley, these 4,000- to 5,000-foot peaks (Kankone Peak is 4,987 feet high, Glacier Peak 4,310 feet) are called the Kantishna Hills.

Although attention at first focused on Chitsia Creek, site of Wickersham's discovery, the fact is that a showing of gold flakes in the prospector's gold pan could have been found in almost any creek in the Kantishna Hills. In the spring of 1904, prospectors converged on the area but spread out to explore all of the creeks. Chitsia Mountain (3,862 feet), anchoring the north end of the Kantishna Hills, divided the Kantishna drainage from that of the

Toklat River to the east. Joe Dalton and a partner prospected the Toklat and found small amounts of gold in 1904. But the creeks that drain down from Wickersham Dome and Glacier Peak on the south end of the range attracted the most attention. Caribou, Glacier, Friday, and Eureka creeks flowed northwest, out of the Kantishna Hills and into the vast and flat lowland plain of the Kantishna and Tanana valleys.[7] During the winter, at least one group of prospectors, led by Tom Gane of Tacoma, went into the Kantishna region and prospected there and over into the headwaters of the Kuskokwim.

Joe Quigley and Jack Horn also set out to prospect the Kantishna Hills in the spring of 1905.[8] Tall, lanky Joe, from Kittanning, Pennsylvania, had been only twenty-two when he ventured north, in the years before the Klondike gold rush. At least, that is what he told Grant Pearson. "I have never forgotten the day I crossed the pass," he told Pearson. "It was the ninth of May, 1891, and my birthday, I was then twenty-two years young."[9] He was known to have been in Fortymile,[10] perhaps as early as 1892, and he was photographed as one of the Yukon Order of Pioneers (YOOP) posing in Dawson City in 1897. The YOOP was formed to honor those who had arrived before the Klondike strike. Jack Horn, who had mined on Hunker Creek (where he had been a neighbor of Fannie's), was also in the photo.

Joe signed out on the Clary Craig post office register in August 1901, headed for Eagle. His name did not show up again in any official records until March 1905, when he filed on claims he had located in the hills surrounding Fairbanks. When he filed on March 6, Joe affirmed that he located No. 1 Above on Jump Off Joe Creek on December 18 and No. 2 Below on 4th of July Creek on December 20. Both creeks are tributaries of the Little Chena River that head within the rich landmass of Pedro Dome, in the area of Fairbanks and Fish creeks, and both are still mined today.

Joe Quigley (#17), Dawson City, 1897, with Yukon Order of Pioneers, evidence that he was in Dawson at the time. *UAF Ralph McKay Collection 1970-0058-00254*

It must have been shortly after he arrived in town and filed on claims that Joe set out for the Kantishna Hills, as the spring days were getting longer and were a prime time for mushing.[12] Spring travel by dog team was far easier than the tortuous trip up the rivers and through the swamps in the summer. Prospecting itself required digging a shaft into permafrost ground; summer or winter, one would have to build a fire and melt out a few feet of dirt at a time. By May 7, 1905, Joe had located Discovery Claim on Caribou Creek. Eventually, he and Horn located and staked claims on Glacier and Caribou creeks. Staking itself required only pounding properly identified stakes into the ground being claimed, but before the claims were legal, someone would have to travel back to Fairbanks to record them. So, as Grant Pearson related the story: "They waited for breakup, built a raft at the fork of the Bearpaw and Kantishna, and floated down to the Tanana and caught a steamer to Fairbanks." By July 10, they were back in Fairbanks and at the recorder's office, where they registered their own claims as well as those of a number of others who had made their way out to the creeks.[13] According to Pearson, their recorded claims, as well as their incidental talk while "showing samples of their coarse gold" as they made their way through the stores and bars of Fairbanks, started a kind of ministampede that had not been seen since the early days in Dawson.

Gold fever burned so hot in Fairbanks that by mid-August, two of the six members of the Fairbanks City Council had left for the Kantishna, and a third was on his way. Meanwhile, in July, after Horn and Quigley had left the area, Joe Dalton and Joe Stiles staked Eureka Creek, which was the first creek to be a major producer in the area.[14] Unfortunately for historians, the editions of the Fairbanks newspapers from the spring of 1905 have all disappeared. By the time an earnest historian can pick up the trail through the microfilm, it is August 1905, and the Fairbanks papers were filled with a steady stream of news about the strike; by August 12, the newspaper reported that all the ground on Glacier, Caribou, Eureka, and Eldorado creeks had been staked. Then, on August 24, Harry Karstens and Charlie McGonagall, "two crack mail carriers," announced plans to carry freight and passengers on an overland winter express route.[15] These two men, both destined to play important roles in the history of the park, had already made their reputations carrying the mail by dog sled on the winter route over the Alaska Range from Fairbanks to Valdez.

Nearly a thousand people rushed into the Kantishna, most by boat. The transportation companies followed Wickersham's route up the Kantishna River to the mouth of the Bearpaw. But the Bearpaw is a river in name only: mostly, it is a tortured, twisted stream, meandering its way through mosquito-infested flats for mile after mile. Passengers returning from the new diggings reported that Dalton was taking out from $500 to $1,000 a day with a rocker on his discovery claim. (A rocker was a gold-sifting device consisting of a box that could be rocked back and forth on rockers like a rocking chair and could be operated by one man with a limited amount of water.) This news prompted the ever enthusiastic reporters to predict, "If all the stories told about the Kantishna are true, and especially the ones about the richness of Eureka Creek, then this country has a gold streak which will discount the wonderful richness of Portland bench in the Nome Country."[16]

In spite of what must have been a difficult journey, the rush seemed a soft one to the old-timers. "It don't seem natural," one old-timer remarked, according to the local newspaper. "It's too tame like. You ride almost to the diggings in upholstered seats on a steamer, and find petticoats all along the line. I kept looking for the telegraph line, and it was hard to realize that I was on a real stampede, such as we used to follow in the old days. I suppose electric cars will soon be whirring up the canyon."[17]

By September 25, the steamer *White Seal* was getting ready to make a last trip in for the season. The transportation company estimated that 1,000 tons of supplies had been hauled in and that there were nearly a thousand people, as well.[18]

The rush persisted through the fall of 1905, but many of the original claims proved shallow and were soon worked out. The most persistent miners continued to prospect and work their claims, even as conflicting stories reached the Fairbanks press. Although some said the ground was worked out, fifty to one hundred miners expected to work through the 1905–06 winter, and those who had staked successful claims the year before put together their outfits and announced plans to return.

Travel was so difficult that temporary settlements sprang up to serve as transshipment points, where would-be miners could cache their goods before beginning the next leg of the trip. Twenty miles up the Bearpaw from the Kantishna River, at the mouth of Moose Creek, freight and passengers had to be off-loaded at Diamond. From that point, travelers had to make their way overland through the swamps to Glacier City, at the mouth of Glacier Creek.

The only evidence I had about when Fannie might have gone into the Kantishna was a letter she wrote to her sister, mailed from Chena, in August 1907: "You see I left Chena year ago last august. I am close to Mount McKinley only 15 miles. . . . I got seed you sent so good by god bless you all write soon your, Mrs. Fannie McKenzie." This letter seemed to say that she had actually left Chena in the fall of 1906, rather than at the beginning of the rush in 1905 as I would have expected.

Not until I did a final search at the recorder's office in January 2006 did I find another key piece of evidence in the microfilm version of the book of deeds. These microfilm copies are not easy to read: when I began my first step, checking the index by last name, I found the list for "Mc" was so poorly copied and so faint that I could hardly read it. But miraculously, something caught my eye and led me to a bill of sale dated December 4, 1905, in Glacier City: "Know all men by these presents," it began in typical fashion, in a sort of shorthand of a florid script that looked indecipherable until I got the hang of it. According to this document, Fannie was selling "right title and interest in Lot 4 block 3, situated in Glacier City" to Robert Gunn and Carl Nelson for the consideration of $190, including a cabin 21 feet by 16 feet. The deed was filed March 12, 1906. So here was evidence that Fannie had established herself in Glacier City early in the rush, following her old pattern of being among the first on the scene. By December, she was already selling out.

All these little tidbits were pieces of a puzzle, and my job was to find a story, a chronological narrative into which all the pieces fit and made sense. But evidence is not always as simple to interpret as it seems. In this case, I believe Fannie wrote the letter from Kantishna sometime in the spring of 1907 and gave it to someone else who finally mailed it from Chena in August 1907. If she wrote the letter in March 1907, she was actually saying that she had left Chena a year before August 1906, in other words, in fall 1905.

Twenty-eight when she arrived in the Klondike in 1898, she had spent five years in Dawson and two and a half in Fairbanks. She was getting older, and it may be that, like many of her fellow stampeders, she was looking for a place to settle down. Or maybe she was trying to put some distance between herself and Angus. After Fannie walked out on him in 1903, he had followed her on the trail to Fairbanks, where he located No. 16 Above on Beaver Creek, a tributary of the South Fork of the Chena River on August 28, 1904.[19] Whether Fannie tried to divorce him or he died is unknown. Perhaps she had indeed met Joe Quigley and, trusting his opinion of his finds, decided the Kantishna was a place where she could really make her stake.

—⁂—

The summer of 1906 saw a renewal of activity in the area. Joe Dalton and his brother, Jim, together with their partners Joe and Simon Stiles, were

Placer Mining

Eons of wasting erosion washed some of the gold hidden in the hills down into the creek beds, where it settled into the valleys with hundreds of feet of gravels. Heavier than the surrounding rock, this is the placer gold, the loose gold flakes and nuggets found in gravel beds; it can be recovered with a gold pan or any of the devices that separate the gold from the gravel. The water that eroded the rock further sifted the gold down through the gravel to lie, finally, just above the bedrock. Further erosion buried the gold and the gravel beneath sometimes 50 or 100 feet of dirt, and in the North, this dirt, or overburden, is frozen year-round as permafrost. Miners in the Klondike and later in Fairbanks had to dig shafts down through the frozen dirt to mine the gold lying just above the bedrock. From the bottom of the shafts, they tunneled out in "drifts," following the course of the ancient stream or the veins of gold.

Rocking for gold. The gold rocker was a step up in technology from the gold pan. It used little water and could be operated by one person. In the background, one of the miners stands ready at the windlass to haul up another bucket of dirt from the mine shaft. *UAF Albert Johnson Photo Collection 89-166-635*

Sluice box. The miner shoveled the pay dirt into the long sluice box, and then creek water running through the box separated the gold from the gravel. Notice the miner, bent over, in the middle of the photo. *UAF Stephen Foster Collection 69-90-599*

This process is called drift mining. Whether the miner uses a primitive gold pan or a gold dredge, whether the gravel is on the surface or deep underground, the process of separating the gold is the same. The gold is heavier than the gravel, and it sinks to the bottom of the pan when washed about with water. From gold pans, miners moved to the rocker, a box on rockers which could be operated by one person, and then to the more common sluice boxes. Early sluices were open boxes that were 10 to 20 feet long and perhaps 1 foot wide and 8 to 12 inches deep. The bottom of the box had riffles nailed every 8 inches or so. The miners shoveled the gravel into the sluice box and then channeled creek water through it to wash out the heavier gold, which was trapped behind the riffles.

Later capitalists bought up hundreds of acres of ground and brought in giant floating gold dredges to dig and sift through the gold by mechanical means. Today, few dredges continue to operate. Miners find it more efficient to use conventional earth-moving equipment such as tractors, loaders, and dump trucks to move the gold-bearing gravel to a stationary wash plant.[20]

"Open-cut work on Little Moose Creek." The sluice box in this photo and the one above are made of local rough-cut lumber and illustrate the primitive type of mining conducted in the Kantishna as late as 1915. *UAF Frederick Drane Collection 91-046-702*

working on their claims on Eureka Creek, and in mid-August 1906, they returned to Fairbanks with $86,000 in gold dust.[21] "KANTISHNA BEATS ALL," was the headline on an August 25 article in the *Fairbanks Evening News*, which described nine large nuggets and $10,000 worth of gold dust found at No. 15 Above on Glacier Creek by A. J. Benbennek and J. H. Benson.[22]

On September 10, Jim Chronister and Billy Abramsky came in from their claims at No. 16 Above Glacier Creek. "While they were non-committal as to the amount brought in as a result of the year's work," stated the newspaper report that day, "it is said the pokes they carried with them would choke an elephant."[23] (A gold poke was a slim caribou skin bag about 10 inches long and 3 or 4 inches in diameter in which the miners carried and stored their gold nuggets and dust.)

Still, others cast doubt on the richness of the district. As Bob Mann, who returned to Fairbanks in early September, explained, "Everyone knows just what the country is who has ever been there, and the men who have struck the right kind of ground think, of course, that the country is all to the good, and a greater number, who failed to find the pay, think contrariwise. But personally, I don't believe that the Kantishna deserves the bad reputation it appears to bear."[24] Nevertheless, by the late summer of 1906, most sources agreed that the rush was over, and the towns of Diamond, Glacier City, and Roosevelt were nearly deserted.

After arriving in the fall of 1905 and putting up her "Meals for Sale" sign in Glacier City, Fannie settled in with Joe Quigley on Glacier Creek in the spring of 1906 and cooked through the winter, just as she had in the small rushes to numerous outlying districts in the Klondike. Her serious pursuit of mining began at that time, and her hopes were high that she might soon realize a profit after her years of effort.

FIVE

Digging In
Mining Claims

MINING WAS THE BACKBONE of the Kantishna community. Though Fannie eventually became famous for her wilderness lifestyle, mining was the focus of her efforts and the reason she stayed in the Kantishna country for nearly forty years, always hoping for a profit from all her years of effort.

Until a few years ago, the recorder's office in Fairbanks housed the musty leather-bound books with the original handwritten mining claim records, written in the order in which they came into the office. The records are organized by an arcane indexing system: on the page for names beginning with *Q,* for example, there is a citation for every claim recorded in that book, with a page number and a claim number. The first time I looked through the records, I was still searching for claims filed by "Fannie Quigley" in 1906, 1907, 1908, or 1909, but there was nothing listed. None of the articles or stories I had read at that point mentioned "Mrs. McKenzie"; rather, all the stories suggested that Fannie had married Joe Quigley in 1906 and gone to Kantishna as his wife. It was some time later that Bill Brown and I found the photo of "Mother M'Kenzie's Cabin on the Kantishna" in Belmore Browne's *Outing Magazine* article from 1913. Who was Mrs. McKenzie, we wondered? If not for the genealogy club of Fairbanks and its efforts to index obituaries in the *Fairbanks Daily News-Miner,* I might not have found the obituary with the line "Nearly everyone remembers her marriage to Angus McKenzie." (Of course, by the time I read that, it seemed no one at all remembered that marriage.) It was not until I went back to the indexes and began looking under "Mc" that I realized that Fannie was an active participant in the mining business from the time of her

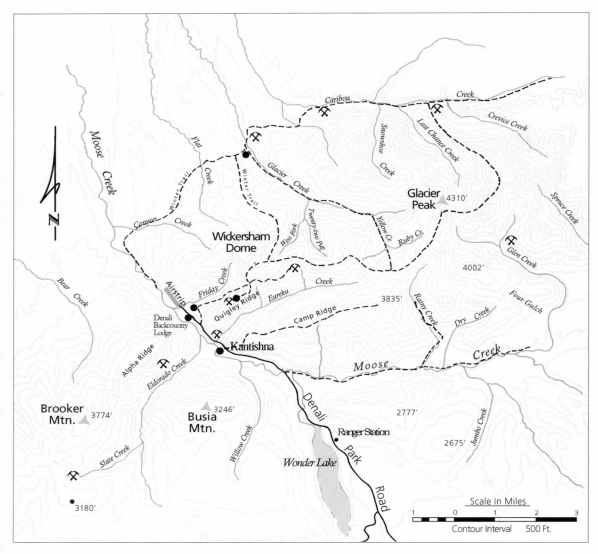

The Kantishna. Fannie's cabin on Friday Creek was on the hillside above the airstrip and the junction of Friday and Moose creeks. The cabin on the Silver Pick claim was high on the south side of Quigley Ridge. The cabin on Glacier Creek was just at the point where the creek leaves the steep-walled canyon on the northern flank of Wickersham Dome. *Map by Karen Farrell*

arrival in the district. In fact, she staked twenty-six claims between 1907 and 1918 as "F. McKenzie," "Fannie McKenzie," or "Mrs. McKenzie."

Reading through the claim books was like traveling back in time, imagining Fannie and Joe and others on the creeks. Each claim had to have a discovery of gold—usually involving the digging of a pit or shaft, panning the gravel, and finding a "show" of gold. Then the claim was measured out and staked. In a remote district such as the Kantishna, one person was designated to take the claim notices to the recorder's office in Fairbanks. (Long-legged Joe Quigley, who could make the 150-mile walk in four or five days, was often chosen.) This person was the agent for the others and probably arrived at the office with a batch of filings. The recorder then copied the

Above: "Mother M'Kenzie's Cabin on the Kantishna."
Photo by Merl La Voy, of the Parker Browne expedition
in 1912, as they visited at the Quigley McKenzie cabin on
Glacier Creek. The photo originally appeared in *Outing
Magazine* in 1913. *UAF Francis P. Farquhar Collection Box
2, Folder 31, p. 394. Right:* Joe Quigley stands by a stone
monument on top of the Kantishna Hills. *NPS-DENA*

legal claim descriptions into his large leather-bound
books, one or more for each mining district.

Joe had filed his original discovery claims on
Caribou Creek and those of Jack Horn and about a
dozen others on July 10, 1905. The claims are
recorded in Fairbanks Record Book No. 6, starting
on page 306 and continuing for many pages. About
thirty claims on both Caribou and Glacier creeks
were filed on that date, the day Quigley and Horn
arrived back in Fairbanks from the Kantishna after
the discovery.

Fannie staked her first claim in the Kantishna on
January 1, 1907: the Texas Bench, on the right limit
of Glacier Creek, opposite No. 14 Above. The claim
was witnessed by J. B. Quigley and filed on April 15,
1907. (Right and left limits, or sides, were determined facing downstream on the creek.) This set a

View up Friday Creek. *UAF Fannie Quigley Photo Collection 80-46-247*

pattern. Mining, like any business, involved specific rules, and a miner's knowledge of the rules and how to work the system could contribute to his or her success. After filing their claims, miners were responsible for performing at least $100 of "assessment work" each year. This requirement limited the number of claims that could be held by an individual, unless that person had enough capital to pay someone else to do a share of the work. If the claim owner failed to complete the work by December 31, the ground was again open to staking. Thus, on January 1, Fannie probably filed on a claim that may have been staked and then abandoned by someone else.

The early mining efforts focused on placer gold, the free gold mixed in with the layers of gravel on top of bedrock in the creek beds. In the narrow creek canyons of the Kantishna Hills, miners used open-cut and ground-sluicing techniques. Accordingly, the upper gravel layer was washed down the channel within a foot or so of bedrock. Then the remaining richer gravels were washed or shoveled into the sluice boxes to separate out the gold. This process was effective for the rich shallow diggings, which the miners worked, but once they had mined out the easy diggings, the backbreaking labor ceased to pay off for the ground that was not so rich.

Fannie mushing firewood in a dress. *UAF Fannie Quigley Photo Collection 80-46-66*

CHASING THE YELLOW PUP

The Fannie Quigley legends have always centered on Friday Creek because Fannie's final home was the small house near the airstrip where Friday Creek joins Moose Creek, about 4 miles downstream from what is left of the minimal townsite of Kantishna. Now transitioning to serve the ecotourists, Kantishna is 90 miles into the park at the end of the Park Road, which was built between 1923 and 1938 through the heart of Denali National Park. But from the time I found Merl La Voy's photo of "Mother M'Kenzie's Cabin," I had always wanted to find the site of Fannie's original home and garden on Glacier Creek. Sleuthing in libraries and archives, I had turned up USGS geologist Stephen Capps's map and field notes from a 1915 trip he took to Kantishna, as well as a photo of Fannie in a long black dress in a fenced garden adjoining a cabin.[1] With its canvas roofing nailed over the edges of the roof and its distinctive log work and proportions, the structure had to be the back of the cabin in the La Voy photo from 1912— Fannie's original roadhouse on Glacier Creek. And on Capps's map was a notation "Q&M"—Quigley & McKenzie—with a dot for a cabin that had to be their place. Capps described visiting Fannie and Joe and detailed the flowers and vegetables growing in Fannie's garden in his field notes. But just how *I* was to get there was a problem. No one had mined the area since the early 1970s, and by the time I began my quest in the early 1990s, not even a trail remained.

The original Denali Backcountry Lodge, now on the banks of Moose Creek, was built in the late 1980s, and when I was invited there to give a talk about Fannie, it seemed the perfect opportunity to pursue my quest. My husband accompanied me as driver, companion, and field assistant, and we decided to take mountain bikes with us, though I am anything but an expert, or even regular rider. The high valleys traversed by the Park Road are magnificently scenic, with the jagged, snow-covered peaks of the Alaska Range rising up to the south. Ancient glaciers formed the gravel outwash plains making up the innumerable valleys of the many braided rivers. The road clings to the Outer Range north of the valleys, which is equally jagged but lower and rockier. Built partly as a mining road but planned according to the same National Park Service design standards as the Blue Ridge Parkway, the road presents a series of dramatic vistas, in addition to hair-raising cliffs and turns. Traveling the road is an adventure, marked by the names of the rivers crossed and the landmark hills and mountains traversed: the Savage, Sanctuary, Teklanika, and Toklat rivers and Cathedral Mountain, Polychrome Pass, and Stony Dome. And then there is the wildlife: Dall sheep inhabit the outer ranges, and caribou, wolves, fox, and grizzly bears roam the valleys.

The lodge was sited on Moose Creek within view of Fannie's old Friday Creek digs. But Fannie never enjoyed such comfortable surroundings. We slept in a Lind Cedar–style snug cabin with running water, a shower, and beds made up with fresh sheets. We ate gourmet food, wonderfully prepared for the sixty or so guests and the young and very hip staff. In my presentation to staff and guests, I tried to explain the life and times of Fannie Quigley, who was born in Nebraska in 1870 and died alone in that shack just a quarter of a mile away, down by the airstrip, in 1944.[2]

After asking around for ideas about how to get to Glacier Creek, my husband and I met a miner who said that he had built the Skyline Road back in 1983 to get to his claims on Caribou Creek. So, following his directions, we left the lodge the next morning, driving the rough mining road up Quigley Ridge and over the shoulder of Wickersham Dome, heading for the head of Yellow Pup[3]—one of the tributaries that form the headwaters of Glacier Creek. For some reason, maybe because I am a historian, I carried only Stephen Capps's hand-drawn 1915 map and not the modern USGS topographic maps.

We followed the road hugging the north side of Quigley Ridge; below us, Friday Creek was just a trickle in the narrow V-shaped valley to our left. We came out at a saddle, where we crossed the ridge as the road began to rise up to Wickersham Dome. South, to our right, we could see down to the next drainage, Eureka Creek, a cleft in the hills and the site of Joe Dalton's discoveries. And beyond the next ridge, the magnificent panorama of the Alaska Range spread out at its most glorious, with Mount McKinley at the western end. With the truck in compound low four-wheel drive, Chris managed to navigate the meanest piece of sharply pitched, boulder-strewn ruts I have ever seen. We chugged along up the hillside as the road continued around the south flank of Wickersham Dome, its tundra-covered rocky slopes rising to 3,500 feet above us. As we crossed over to the east flank of the dome, a branch road took off down a north spur of the hill and into a creek marked on the map as Twenty-two Gulch (named after the number of the claim where the gulch joins Glacier Creek). Far down near the creek, we could see a white spot that we identified through binoculars as a camper left by a more recent miner, testimony to the fact that there was once some kind of a road down there.

Continuing on, we followed the ridgeline around to the headwaters of Glacier Creek. Just as our directions indicated, far down a nearly sheer canyon to the left we saw Yellow Pup, recognizable from the exposed gravels indicating areas that had been extensively mined. We stopped and unloaded our bikes at the head of an old road leading precipitously down into the valley. It was too steep even to ride, so we began our trip walking our bikes down and trying not to think about having to walk them up again. Reddish, iron-stained mineral seeps emerged from places in the rocky banks of the headwaters of the stream. When we reached the main creek, we came to a road partly leveled by a tractor in some previous mining venture.

Glacier Creek watershed heads in an amphitheater of rocky, tundra-covered hillsides dominated by the 4,310-foot Glacier Peak, which continues in sharp ridges to the north, the sides of the hills descending into a valley so tight it is almost a canyon. The country is so dry that it is surprising not that the creek is small but that it flows out of the rocky hillsides at all. Following the overgrown road down Yellow Pup, we came to the point where the tributary joins the main branch of Glacier Creek, heading from the next hillside cleft.

Descending through the valley on our bikes, we spotted our first old cabin site. The cabin rose out of the willows and alders on a natural bench on the north side of the creek, where a widening of the walled canyon created the only available spot for habitation. The cabin was fallen in, with only bits of the floor and a piece of the ridge pole visible. Lengths of sheet metal grown over with weeds clunked underfoot. Nearby, we found a small level field, which must have once been a garden site, now overgrown with purple fireweed and dark blue delphinium gone wild. The site was somehow both desolate and yet, with its signs of habitation, intimately personal. Scattered pieces of plywood indicated that it had been reinhabited during the mining boom of the 1970s and then abandoned once again. Climbing down the hillside bench to the creek, we were startled by a lone caribou in the canyon who, startled himself, bounded up the hill to avoid us.

Many creek claims were staked during the original rush, though most were soon abandoned. But to ensure they would get in on any deals in case the area really did turn out to be rich, the remaining miners joined in the general staking of nearly all the ground in the Glacier and Caribou creek watersheds in association claims, whereby a large piece of ground could be staked by a group of prospectors. The associations included, in various combinations, most of the prospectors and miners left in the area, including Fannie, and eventually claimed the majority of the ground, though little came of the effort. Unlike creek claims, which were numbered, the associations always had colorful names.

For example, on January 1, 1908, J. B. Quigley, W. R. Taylor, Charles McGonagall, Thomas Lloyd, F. McKenzie, H. Karstens, James Sedlacek, and U. J. Paxson staked a 160-acre association claim called the New York Group on Glacier Creek at the lower end of claim No. 12 Above and running downstream. (Like many other miners, Fannie may have staked a claim for another by power of attorney.) Quigley filed as agent on March 25, 1908. The Canyon Association and the January, February, and March Associations followed on Caribou Creek. Then came the Timber Line Association, the Blue Association, the White Association, and the Portland Association. Fannie was a part of all of them.

For all the claiming activity, there was little to see on the hillsides as we hiked and biked down another mile to Twenty-two Gulch. But evidence of an old road was clear. In places, we could even ride our bikes a few hundred yards, coasting gently down, but for the most part, the road was full of boulders, and it crossed and recrossed the creek; in some places, many places, the creek had chosen to follow the road, and we splashed through it, down it, until the road took off by itself again into the brush.

Twenty-two Gulch was a wide junction of streams much disturbed by recent mining, and there, the lone, forlorn camper we had spotted was parked and the road ended. Glacier Creek continued down again through a narrow cleft, and our choice was either to wade through the creek or traverse the nearly vertical slope, bushwhacking through the blueberries, ripe and abundant during those last days of July. Because the weather was as hot and muggy as Charles Sheldon had described it in 1907 during this same two-week period, we chose the creek. Surprisingly, there were few mosquitoes.

On Capps's 1916 mining survey, he had noted that "the uppermost claim on which mining was done in 1916 is claim Number 20 Above, situated 1-1/2 miles above the point at which Glacier Creek emerges from the mountains." He reported that two men were sluicing gravel there, with sluice boxes set on grade. Since this was the claim Fannie had staked on January 20, 1914, the men were probably working it on a lease. Capps had reported that "the gold is coarse but is said to be unevenly distributed rich spots being surrounded by lean areas in which there is insufficient gold to pay the cost of mining." We were probably traversing the area that had been mined in 1914, but there was little evidence of mining activity.[4]

Shortly, the creek's canyon widened again, and after going around a few more bends, we could look up at the ridges coming down from Wickersham Dome. Across the creek, on the northwest side, we found another cabin. It was a nice site, a high gravel bar or low bench, only 3 or 4 feet above the streambed, in a field of fireweed. I tried to imagine that this was Fannie's cabin, the "Q&M," or Quigley-McKenzie, cabin on Capps's 1916 map. But was it?

The cabin was constructed with vertical corner posts. The horizontal logs making up the front were nailed into the corner posts, and the joints were covered with vertical board trim, also holding on a canvas covering. At least we could see where the canvas had been attached, from the shreds of it still remaining. This, at least, matched the photo of Fannie's cabin in 1913. The roof, of course, had fallen in and disappeared. Inside, among the weeds, we found the wood cookstove, and outside, we spotted the warming shelf that would have stood above it. On a table made of rough boards sat various artifacts already arranged by previous visitors: a few dishes, bread pans, a hand-cranked forge, pieces of harness. The forge reminded me of a later prospector's description of his first meeting with Fannie in the 1940s. The first thing she did, he reported, was to insist on sharpening his pick in a small forge in her cabin. Digging around in the grass under the table, I had just discovered the remains of a boot—small enough to be a woman's, I thought—when a yellow jacket stung me and ended that avenue of exploration. In my mind, the cabin, the level spot for the garden, and the creek in front made the picture I wanted to see. I was hot and tired, and my legs ached. I wanted this to be Fannie's cabin.

Geologist Stephen Capps had stayed with Fannie and Joe that summer of 1916 and described the site: the claim was on bench, with a "steep face 40 feet high at the creek edge." Where was the steep bench? The hillside rising so sharply behind the cabin did not match the photo, and our cabin site was on the opposite side of the creek from the location identified by Capps. I knew the map indicated that the Quigley-McKenzie cabin was out beyond the tight canyon, where the creek emerged from the hills. Out of time, needing to start back, thinking with dread of the climb back up Yellow Pup, I desperately wanted this to be Fannie's cabin, but I knew it was not. Later, looking more closely at Capps's map, we saw that the cabin we had found was also there—not Fannie's but clearly placed in a bend upstream from No. 14 Above. I would have to plan another expedition.

GLACIER CREEK, 1994 AND 1995

When I was invited again to the Backcountry Lodge, right on Moose Creek in Kantishna, to talk about Fannie Quigley, my obsession with finding her Glacier Creek cabin returned. As my husband and I drove into the lodge, I saw the tourists with head nets on. I laughed. Silly tourists! But I soon found out it was no joke. It was the first week of June, and the mosquitoes, newly hatched, were ferocious. A short hike after dinner had me in a frenzy of slapping and dancing through the tundra in the evening light.

The lodge staff told us that Sonny, the miner from Caribou Creek, had been hired by the Park Service to retrieve and dispose of all the old mining equipment, the junk, and the trash left on miles of Caribou and Glacier creeks through the 1970s and 1980s; in the process, he had pushed through a new tractor trail across the tundra from the airstrip, over the shoulder of Wickersham Dome to Glacier Creek. Fearing that this track would mire us in swamp and bog and with the mosquitoes so thick we had to wear head nets ourselves, Chris and I decided against trying it.

Instead, we again drove up the miners' Skyline Road to the top of Wickersham Dome, to try following the long ridge down to the creek, which we had seen the year before. The road, bone jarring and filled with boulders, was worse than before. But the view from the top of the dome spread out in its own timeless way before us. To the northwest was nothing, or so it seemed: a valley so broad it looked like the ocean. The long fingers of the ridges descended from the dome and spread out into a valley floor, which extended flat 100 miles out to the horizon.

We left the truck and started our descent to the northeast of the dome on foot over tundra bouncy with deep moss. Too late to correct our course, we realized we had headed down too far to the northeast, and as we neared the creek, we met the alders, the shrubby trees that grow in disturbed ground. "Alder Hell," the guides from the lodge called it—alders growing up in a dense and twisted mass, their trunks nearly parallel to the hill and aimed roughly downhill so that to go down is treacherous but to go across or uphill is nearly impossible. These are alders that can hide bears near the creek beds, alders so dense they lead directly to angry outbursts and re-criminations ("I told you we should have gone the other way!" "If we had just crossed the creek farther up we could have avoided this altogether!").

But we somehow continued, descending the long finger of the ridge until we reached a cabin the guides had told us about, "Fuksa's," a plywood shack perched on a ledge above the creek, dating from the mining renaissance of the 1970s. We went in for a respite from the mosquitoes. Not exactly abandoned, it was full of minimal housekeeping essentials and old magazines. Outside, the creek bubbled in its rocky gulch, taunting us.

Leaving, we passed the generator shed, crossed the small tributary gulch on a rough plank, and climbed back up onto the ridge above to follow the creek downstream. But the side hill was so steep my knees and ankles and feet hurt traversing it. Finally, in desperation, we descended and waded down Glacier Creek itself as it burbled through the willow-covered rocky walls of the narrow canyon in a series of rocky pools and riffles. The icy cold, clear water immediately numbed my aching feet and knees, but there was no hint of gold. Soon, we came to a penstock, or small dam, which had once im-pounded the creek to send the water into a pipe flume.

By 1916, ten years after he had begun mining the claim No. 14 Above, Capps noted, Quigley had built a ditch that tapped Glacier Creek "at the lower end of claim Number 16." This, I realized, had to be the penstock for that flume. In fact, though Quigley owned claims No. 13 and half of No. 14, Fannie by then was the owner of No. 16 Above, a worked-out claim but essential to the ditch system Joe was using to mine No. 14. She had again taken advantage of the magic expiration date, staking it on January 1, 1916.

Around the next bend, I thought, around the next bend, as we struggled through the creek, hanging onto willows to keep our footing. And we did finally emerge from the tight bends of the canyon, to a wider spot with a high bench above the creek to our left. Across from it, to our right, was a modern-looking plywood cabin. We headed for the cabin to get away from the mosquitoes. Jahoula's cabin, like Fuksa's, built in the 1970s as the price of gold reached $800 per ounce, had obviously at one time been lived in for long periods. From the small window facing the creek, we could see the bench on the other side, a small plateau, perhaps 40 feet above the creek and just at the base of the last ridge descending from the high slopes of Wickersham Dome—just where the "Q&M" dot was on Capps's map.

Capps had described the mining technique that was used in the area: "Mining was done by running successive cuts from the ditch to the edge of the bench, and the tailings were discharged over the bench into Glacier Creek." Later, looking at a photo of the claim, we could see the lines of these successive cuts, visible as gashes through the vegetation. "The bench gravels that were worked are said to have yielded a good profit to the miners," Capps had said, "but the increasing depth of the ground and the difficulties encountered in keeping the ditch in repair so increased the costs that no mining on the bench has been done for several years."[5]

Leaving Jahoula's, we crossed the creek and picked an eroded gully to climb up to that high bench. We reached the plateau only to find ourselves again in Alder Hell. Uneven gravel ridges that we stumbled over indicated that the whole bench had been mined, which accorded with the description. But the entire area was grown up in 10-foot alders so dense that if there had been a cabin, we would not have seen it. Following hints of old roads, we came to a shack that appeared to be newer than any cabin Fannie and Joe would have had at this location, perhaps from the 1930s. It was partly, really mostly, fallen in, and it had a sign, "WARNING—EXPLOSIVES STAY OUT." I was convinced. Pushing our way through the alders in back of the shack, we stumbled on an abandoned yellow bulldozer. The alders were so thick the dozer could not be seen from more than 5 feet away. Climbing up on top of it, we hoped to see the lay of the land, get an idea of where the Quigley cabin might have been, but it was impossible.

Twenty-five feet directly south of the cabin was the tractor trail Sonny had made the previous winter. Resigning ourselves to our anticlimactic discovery and again with barely enough time to get back to the lodge for din-

ner and my next talk, we followed Sonny's trail up to the shoulder of the ridge. There on the ridge, I fell exhausted onto the spongy moss of the tundra. From that height, I could look back down, down to the high bench overlooking Glacier Creek, down to follow the creek as it flowed between the fingers of the ridges and out into the flats. Even though we could not exactly locate the cabin, I could at last picture the site. It was a good site for a roadhouse, halfway between the river landing and the claims upstream and over the dome. It was a site that would be easy to access, and easy to haul wood from down by the Bearpaw River; it was a site out of the tight canyon, where the sun would come early in the spring—a site good for gardening. I could picture it.

By 1918, travelers to the Kantishna reported that little placer work had been done since at least 1915. The placer ground on Glacier was nearly worked out, with decreasing profit to show for any effort put in. But by that time, of course, Joe and Fannie had staked many hard rock claims on Quigley Ridge and had moved the base of their operations.

SIX

Hard Rock

Quigley Ridge and Friday Creek

MARRIAGE

ON FEBRUARY 2, 1918, Fannie McKenzie and Joe Quigley were officially married by J. C. Van Orsdel, commissioner for the Kantishna Recording District, at his residence on Glacier Creek. So says the copy of the marriage certificate I received from the Bureau of Vital Statistics, despite the many references to Fannie as Mrs. Quigley that appeared as early as 1907. This leaves us with the fact, uncomfortable for some, that Joe and Fannie were simply cohabiting for those twelve years. Charles Sheldon, a big-game hunter from New York, said as much in his journal when he met Fannie in Joe's cabin in 1907, and Joe and Fannie traveled out to hunt with Sheldon later in 1908.[1] Fannie's story is a classic case of the times and values of the period during which the story was told influencing the story itself. In spite of evidence and probably individual recollections to the contrary, writers such as Grant Pearson wanted to portray Fannie in what they perceived to be a positive light, reflecting the values of the 1940s and 1950s. Thus, in the story as most often told, Fannie was married to Joe when she left with him for Kantishna.[2] In fact, however, Fannie maintained her individuality and referred to herself during this period as Mrs. McKenzie. For instance, she operated a roadhouse in the Kantishna that was known as "Mother McKenzie's Cabin," pictured, captioned, and described in the article by Belmore Browne in 1913. She also staked a number of claims under the name Fannie McKenzie. She signed letters as Mrs. McKenzie during this period as well. The newspaper in Nenana referred to her as Fannie McKenzie, "a well-known old-timer," as late as January 1918.[3]

ORIGINAL CERTIFICATE OF MARRIAGE FOR FILING WITH UNITED STATES COMMISSIO...
(Contracting parties' copies should be on *Form 3a*, which is the same as the body of this form.)

UNITED STATES OF AMERICA
TERRITORY OF ALASKA

This Certifies That

Joseph Buffington Quigley and *Fannie McKenzie*

of *Eureka Creek* of *Eureka Creek*

WERE UNITED BY ME IN

Holy Matrimony

On the *Second* Day of *February*, In the Year of Our Lord One Thousand

Nine Hundred and *Eighteen* at *Commissioners Residence – Glacier Creek*

And within thirty days this certificate will be filed by me for record with the U. S. Commissioner for the *Fairbanks* Recording Precinct, Territory of Alaska

WITNESSES: *A. L. Van Orsdel* *J. C. Van Orsdel*
J. C. Van Orsdel *U. S. Commissioner*

Clerical or Official Title.

The above CERTIFICATE OF MARRIAGE was filed for record in my office on the *2nd* day of *Feb.* 19*18*, and has been duly recorded by me in Book No. *1*, RECORD OF CERTIFICATES OF MARRIAGES, at page *1*, *Fairbanks* Precinct *Glacier Creek* Div'n No. *4*, Alaska. Registered No. *1*
J. C. Van Orsdel
United States Commissioner.

TERRITORIAL REGISTRAR'S OFFICE, JUNEAU, ALASKA
This CERTIFICATE OF MARRIAGE received APR 23 1918
Entered in Book No. *1*, RECORD OF MARRIAGES
Clerk to Registrar.

N. B.—This original CERTIFICATE OF MARRIAGE after completion, is required by law to be filed within thirty days, by the person solemnizing the marriage, with the nearest United States Commissioner of the precinct in which the marriage was performed. The fees for filing and recording the certificate are those prescribed by the Attorney General of the United States, and the person solemnizing the marriage is required by law to collect the amount for fees from the contracting parties; if he fails or neglects to do so he must pay the fees from his own money.

MARGIN RESERVED FOR BINDING. Write Plainly, With Unfading Ink.—This is a Permanent Record.

Joe and Fannie's marriage certificate, 1918. State of Alaska, Vital Statistics

Why did Joe and Fannie wait so long to get married? And why, after so many years, did they decide to get married just then? When I began to puzzle over these twin dilemmas, my first thought was that perhaps that was when Angus had died. Fannie's first husband, William Angus McKenzie, had followed her to Fairbanks, as did most of the independent population of Dawson. He was in Fairbanks for a time, resident at Pioneer Hotel. By 1910, he had moved on to the Iditarod District, where he was one of the discoverers at No. 1 Above on Otter Creek.[4] I searched for a death certificate in Alaska and in the Yukon but to no avail. I wondered if I could disprove the theory by finding any reference to a divorce. So, on a trip to Juneau, I made my way to the State Archives and looked through the early Fairbanks court records. In fact, divorce was neither unknown nor inconceivable at the time, even for an Irish Catholic woman: I found the record of the 1906 divorce of Belinda Mulrooney from the sniggling Quebecois champagne salesman Charles Charbonneau, who embezzled her fortune.[5] (Ironically, the famous pair had married in Dawson City on the same day as Fannie and Angus.) But I found no record of a divorce of Angus and Fannie

McKenzie. And so the question of why the marriage took place when it did will probably remain a mystery.

Fannie had endured years of loneliness and isolation since her move to the Kantishna in 1905, possibly due to her feelings about her ambiguous social status. As she wrote in a letter to Charles Sheldon in 1913, "I went to Fairbanks last fall. that was my first trip to town in seven years. I didn't see woman for three years. I tell you, I got lonsome. I have not seen automobile yet."[6] This document itself brings up even more questions. Fannie was an able traveler in the North, so why did she never leave Kantishna? Was she simply too busy? Or did she perhaps fear running into Angus? In fact, after 1916, other women were almost continuously resident in Kantishna, including Mrs. Van Orsdel, wife of the commissioner; Paula Anderson, who, with her husband, had a fox farm and roadhouse at Wonder Lake; and Mrs. Ed. Brooker, wife of a later commissioner. Local lore has it that Fannie never got along with any of these women.[7] However, on February 19, 1916, she was inducted into the Pioneer Women of Alaska, a social and benevolent organization in Fairbanks.[8] This also seems to have been the beginning of a more social period in her life. Fannie began to visit Fairbanks and Nenana more frequently.

Whatever the reason they tied the knot, the marriage ushered in a new era of prosperity for Fannie and Joe. After years of seemingly fruitless work on their placer claims, they had relocated to Quigley Ridge, on one of the most promising of the hard rock claims into which Joe had poured time, effort, and money for the previous five years and on which Joe and Fannie had pinned their hopes. The federal government had at last begun construction of the Alaska Railroad, after years of study and much hue and cry about Alaska's transportation needs. Fannie and Joe and their neighbors were among those hoping to benefit directly. Along with the chosen corridor for the railroad from Seward to Fairbanks was an implicit promise by the federal government to construct connecting roads and trails.

HARD ROCK CLAIMS

The experienced miners fanning out across the Kantishna were well aware that the high and rocky hills there were similar in height, steepness, and geology to many of the mineral-bearing hills in the Yukon, especially those in the Stewart River area, and in Mayo, the area close to Fannie's old claim on Clear Creek, which was being developed as a rich silver-mining area. They noticed the nuggets of lead-silver ore in their sluice boxes and began prospecting and filing hard rock claims. But getting at these minerals locked

Hard Rock Mining

Hard rock mining involves mining lode minerals as they are found as a mineral component of surrounding rock or in veins of quartz, just as it had been intruded into faults or fractures by ancient volcanic activity. Minerals such as galena, as mined by the Quigleys, contained significant amounts of silver and lead as well as gold. Lode miners must tunnel into the hillsides or cut them away in strip-mining operations and then crush the ore to extract the gold through chemical processing.

A hard rock mine used a mill to crush the rock ore, thus allowing for chemical processes to work to separate out the gold. The early mines used stamp mills: each stamp weighed half a ton and was lifted through electric or steam power and allowed to fall on the ore to crush it. Later, more sophisticated operations, including the modern Fort Knox mine outside of Fairbanks, used a large ball mill, resembling a giant rotating clothes dryer filled with iron balls that crushed the ore.

up in veins within the rock of the hillsides would be a much more difficult, technical, and time-consuming process.

Like the association claims, the lode claims were known by the colorful names dreamed up by the miners. Fannie herself had filed her first lode claim, the Midnight Lode, in May 1907. Meanwhile, Tom Lloyd and partners prospected the Glen Creek Drainage, on the south side of the ridge, and eventually developed an antimony deposit on Slate Creek. By 1916, the Lloyd group was shipping 125 tons of ore. Lloyd and his partners were the men who, through their continued presence in the district, hard work, and many trips ferrying supplies, had determined several years earlier that they could make a successful climb of Mount McKinley. Accordingly, Tom Lloyd, William Taylor, Charlie McGonagall, and Pete Anderson formed the Sourdough Expedition, and they successfully climbed the North Peak of McKinley in the spring of 1910.

While Lloyd and the others staked Glen and Slate creeks, Joe Quigley was prospecting on the steeply sloping ridge between Eureka and Friday creeks that would become known as Quigley Ridge. In November 1910, Joe located his Silver Pick claim, high on the south side of the ridge. That same week, Fannie and Joe together located the Hard Luck Association claim in the same area, on the left fork of Friday Creek, not far away, and Quigley located the Golden Eagle claim on Friday Creek at the same time.

Fannie and Joe continued to live on Glacier Creek, while beginning serious work on their hard rock claims on the ridge. As Fannie explained in her 1913 letter to Charles Sheldon: "We have a cabin on the hill between Eureka and Friday [creeks]. Joe is working on some quartz. One can set in window and see Mt. McKinley and sheep hills. We live up there in the winter and down here in summer."[9]

Because this letter to Sheldon was easily accessible in the University of Alaska Archives in Fairbanks, it was one of the first communications from

Fannie that I ever saw. At the time, I was unfamiliar with the geography, and I did not really stop to think about where exactly the cabins she referred to might be. I had seen various photos of Fannie standing in front of various cabins, but I did not stop to think about tying photographs to specific claim locations and locations on the hills. I assumed that she and Joe had moved in 1918 from Glacier Creek to the familiar Friday Creek cabin on the high bench at the west end of Quigley Ridge, overlooking Friday and Moose creeks, even though a part of my mind knew that there is no view of Mount McKinley from that site.

It was 2005 before I finally had the chance to investigate. By that time, I had the claims maps, the photos, and the description. Cultural resources specialist Jane Bryant has spent the winters at park headquarters studying these things since the late 1990s, and she was someone I could consult and compare notes with. In particular, we had a photo that I had always thought showed the back of the cabin overlooking Friday Creek. In the photo, two women are greeting Fannie at the door of a cabin, and there is snow on the ground. The cabin has a door on the right and, to the left of the door, a peculiar and identifiable, horizontally oriented rectangular window. We knew that Stephen Foster had taken the photo between 1915 and 1919, the period in which he was traveling in the region. And we now recognized the two other women as the young widow Ruth Wilson and her companion Nan Robertson, who traveled to the Kantishna in the fall of 1919. Was it, in fact, an early photo of the Friday Creek cabin? If not, where was the picture taken? Was it perhaps the mysterious site referred to in 1913? We could see in the photo that this was definitely a cabin that Fannie was living in, a place inhabited and domesticated. Somehow, we both alighted on the idea that the Silver Pick claim was the location of the mysterious cabin and possibly the site Fannie had referred to as "up there" in her 1913 letter.

In fact, Chris and I had seen the remains of some kind of shack high up on the Quigley Ridge the first time we went to Kantishna in our old Volkswagen Bus, with two young children in tow. I had talked the Park Service into giving me a historian's permit to drive into the park. The Park Service was conducting a survey of some sort, and we camped at their spot on the north side of Friday Creek. The next morning, we headed down the hill and crossed the creek, and then bushwhacked up the ridge. I had baby Molly in a backpack, and Chris carried four-year-old Anna on his shoulders through the alders. The hillside was steep, the mining remains mysterious. I remember that when we got to the top, we found some sort of shack. But without reference to claim maps or topographical maps, the site remained very vague

in my memory. Just getting to Kantishna always seems to be a minor expedition, and so, over the years, we visited other places in the hills but never made it back to the top of Quigley Ridge.

This time, Jane Bryant and I were determined to answer the specific question we had posed, and we were well armed for the task. I had the claim maps and the USGS topo maps as well as a copy of Stephen Capps's hand-drawn map from his trip in 1916. Jane had the collection of photos: the one taken in 1916 by Stephen Foster and a few other choice items that had been donated to the park in recent years. Park cultural resources director Ann Kain brought her GPS, and Chris came along for the hike. After breakfast at the Backcountry Lodge, we headed out, this time going back up the Kantishna road to the Skyline Road and then up the drive to the beginning of the new trail—a social trail, Jane and Ann called it, made informally by the continued activities of the visitors to the new wilderness lodges. The new trail now headed nearly straight up the west face of the ridge at about a 60° angle, just about right to reach out off the trail at waist level and grab a few blueberries as we passed. It was raining, so we had our rain pants on, but as a result, we sweated enough to get soaking wet anyway.

The top of the ridge consists of a series of rocky outcrops of the general country rock, the Birch Creek schist that forms the ridge and provides the background to the mineral-bearing veins and stringers that have been intruded into it. Where the trail crosses the outcrops, the soft rock has been ground down into glittery sand because of all the mica in it. Joe's efforts

Fannie *(right)* is pictured in a Stephen Foster photo in front of the Silver Pick Cabin, high up on the south side of Quigley Ridge, with visitors Mrs. Ruth Wilson and her companion Nan Robertson in the winter of 1919. Stephen *Foster Collection UAF 1969-0092-00722* over the years focused on identifying the signs of these veins in the surface outcrops and then attempting to follow them through trenches and tunnels. So although we were following a rocky, mostly tundra-covered ridge, which would have had a view of the Alaska Range and Mount McKinley on a clear day, the terrain was marked with what seemed to be random cuts and pits. Playing historian, my first efforts were to somehow orient myself to the terrain, the topography, and the claims. Initially, we found a few of Joe's original claim markers, substantial stone and concrete constructions, and then some more recent survey markers, but no matter how I twisted and turned the map, I could not get the correlation with a particular site. Nonetheless, we continued on the trail along the ridge until we came to the largest of the mining scars, an area that looked blasted out of the south side high on the ridge. And just below it, we saw the edge of the roof of some kind of shack.

Sliding down the sandy schist of the mining scar, we all made it down the 75 or 100 feet to the level of the shack. It was only a 6-foot-by-8-foot frame building. Chris and I remembered this as the structure we had found on our first trip seventeen years before, and sure enough, it had the faint remains of the wallpapering of magazine pages that we vaguely remembered. It had obviously been a workshop of some kind. It was generally surrounded by alders, but there was a sort of a clearing in front, an area cleared either for mining or for a garden, now grown up in grasses. Jane got out the photos, and we realized that what we were seeing was half of a structure that had once been two similar, perhaps identical, back-to-back shacks. And we saw now why we had never made the connections with the pictures before. The two back-to-back shacks together had been an outbuilding located west of a home cabin. Sure enough, making our way beyond the shack through more overgrown alders 50 feet to the northeast, we found the remains in the earth of a square, dugout foundation, just a foot or two deep at the deepest on what would have been the northeast corner of the cabin. Studying the photos, we could indeed see that the cabin pictured had been sunk into the ground.

There were no remains of the cabin, just a rusty shovel that Chris found buried under a few inches of leaves under the alders. But east of the cabin site was another clearing, perhaps a garden or a dog yard or a stand of grass to cut for dog bedding.

The primary photo that Jane referred to showed the cabin homesite from the west, with an outline of the high ridges to the east. So we retreated to a spot as close as possible to where the earlier photo might have been taken, and from there, Jane was able to identify the ridges in the background to her satisfaction. And with that, we satisfied ourselves that "up there" was a small cabin on the Silver Pick claim that faced the magnificent view just as Fannie had said, whereas "down here" referred to the Glacier Creek cabin, where Fannie continued to garden in the summers.

The choice made sense from one point of view. High on the south side of the ridge would have been a much warmer and sunnier spot than down on Glacier Creek on the north side of a ridge because, just as in Fairbanks, the cold air masses in the winter tend to fall to the bottom of the valleys. Of course, that confronted us with yet more questions: How did Fannie and Joe get food, fuel, and water up to the high ridge? And if they were living on the Silver Pick in winters as late as 1919 or even 1920, when did they begin living at Friday Creek? From other photos, it seems that the Friday Creek site was well developed by 1922. We do not have answers to these questions yet. Perhaps more sources will come to light to help us out.

During the 1970s, as the price of gold reached over $700 per ounce, there was a renewed modern mining rush. As long as the area was controlled by miners, it was private property, off limits to tourists and the Park Service. Then, when the Alaska National Interest Lands Conservation Act (ANILCA) was passed, the name of the park was changed from Mount McKinley to Denali National Park and the mining district was incorporated into new Denali National Park and Preserve. For five years, the Park Service continued to issue mining permits. But in 1985, the Sierra Club won an injunction requiring the Park Service to shut down mining. Although miners were theoretically able to submit action plans to receive a permit, no significant mining was ever permitted after 1985. And unable to mine, most claim owners eventually agreed to sell out to the Park Service. Ironically, now that most of the area is under direct park control, the cultural resources are even more endangered.

Now that visitors staying in the lodges are guided on nearly daily hikes, they have created a series of what the Park Service calls "social trails," trails that were not in existence on our earlier visit. As much as the environmental community emphasizes pristine natural surroundings, old mining sites and their crumbling remains have an undeniable lure. Visitors often wonder if these sites are just abandoned or if the Park Service "cares about" the stuff lying around.

Many will come to the conclusion that it does not: after all, if it did, would it not just collect the material itself? The fact is that the Park Service does indeed care for these resources, and sites such as this one have been surveyed, listed, and surveyed again for possible protection in case of wildfires. As part of the Interior Department, the Park Service administers laws on cultural preservation such as the National Register of Historic Places, and thus, it must make sure to follow the rules itself. But its concern is expressed precisely by leaving the sites intact and the remains in place. In the timescale of history, it was only yesterday that the miners walked out, leaving everything behind. If visitors cooperate and leave things as they find them, then these sites will remain intact to enchant and mystify visitors for years to come.

Still free for the taking, however, are the abundant blueberries. And the ridge is covered with them: in mid-July, they were the biggest berries and in the thickest patches I have ever seen. So as we headed back up to the top of the ridge and continued east on the trail, we had to pick a few quarts when we stopped for lunch. It was impossible not to think about the many, many, summers that Fannie picked these same berries, gallons of them, and stored them in Joe's mining tunnels.

And that was where we all noticed how much the shrubs and brush have grown since Fannie and Joe established their homesites there. In all of the photos, the surroundings are tundra: the moss, blueberry, and shrub willow are only 1 or 2 feet high. Now, even in undisturbed areas, the shrubs are 3 to 4 feet tall in many places. The trail we had followed continued east, finally joining up with the faint remains of a road or wagon track to a junction with the Skyline Road at the saddle leading to the top of Wickersham Dome. But we headed back down to Moose Creek and were exhausted when we returned.

—⁂—

The value of the claims on Quigley Ridge must have been convincing. Joe and Fannie each owned many claims, and they continued to do the required assessment work. By January 1914, they had made a decision to officially divide their interests in certain claims. Fannie got the Little Annie Claim, and Joe got the Silver Pick. And throughout 1915, they continued staking new claims. Fannie staked the Aunt Mary Lode claim on the left limit of Friday Creek in January and the Never Sweat Lode, between Eureka and Friday creeks, in May. Meanwhile, Joe filed on the White Hawk, the Martha Q, and the Keystone, all on Quigley Ridge. Then, in November 1916, Fannie filed on No. 1 on Iron Gulch, and Joe filed on the Pittsburgh Lode in the same area. Branching out, Fannie filed on the Montana Lode in March 1917 at the head of Glacier Creek, between Glacier and Yellow Pup; this was near the area of Charlie McGonagall's claims, which he had been successfully working.

While Joe and Fannie both continued to stake the hard rock claims on Quigley Ridge, Fannie also continued to stake new placer claims branching out to Friday and Eureka creeks, as well as keeping up with the claims on Glacier. Joe continued the development work on the lode claims, but Fannie was probably the one who panned out gold for grocery money and other necessities from the small amounts of remaining unworked ground on the otherwise worked-over claims. On January 1, 1916, Fannie again took advantage of the magic expiration date and staked No. 1 Above on Eureka Creek. This claim had originally belonged to Joe Dalton, the discoverer, and had been worked continuously since 1905. Although Capps believed that Eureka had been worked out, he also said there were patches of gravel left by the original miners that might have contained considerable placer. Ever vigilant for ground not already claimed, Fannie filed a discovery claim on Lucky Gulch, a small tributary of Eureka Creek, on July 20, 1917. The fact that she staked on both Glacier and Eureka creeks at that time shows her intention to continue the work on Glacier Creek while also beginning to establish a small operation on Eureka.

Joe's development work consisted of the painstaking hand digging of ditches and tunnels on his properties, using pick and shovel to intersect and then follow the mineralized veins. To determine the probable worth of the ground, mineral samples had to be assayed through chemical processes. Far from any assay office, Joe learned to do his own work, crushing the ore and

Fannie in front of a mining tunnel, probably at the Little Annie mine. *UAF Fannie Quigley Photo Collection 80-46-109*

then weighing, processing, and measuring it. By the time of Capps's 1916 survey, Joe had dug a large number of open cuts on his Pennsylvania and Keystone prospects, attempting to find the course of a large quartz vein nearly 3 feet thick at its outcropping on the Keystone. On the Gold King prospect, he had dug two tunnels, one 30 feet long and the other only 7 feet long, searching for the continuation of a 4-foot-wide quartz vein. On the Golden Eagle were several open cuts and a 145-foot-long tunnel. The vein, though narrow, was said to assay several hundred dollars to the ton, a considerable stake. But in 1918 and 1919, it was the Little Annie on which they focused their hopes. Joe had developed a number of open cuts and a tunnel that encountered the vein 90 feet from the portal. From there, he pushed out a drift 42 feet long.[10]

Joe and Fannie continued to maintain their residence on Glacier Creek, where Fannie kept her garden going while Joe worked on the hard rock claims from which they hoped to see some real gains. By 1918, Joe had been working on those claims for at least six years. He had dug tunnels, assayed veins, and proved up on the rich silver-lead ore he had found on Quigley Ridge. This was what the lingo of the day termed the development work. The minerals were there, and getting them out of the ground was not the problem. The biggest obstacle to success was moving the recovered ore out of the Kantishna country. Like most prospectors, Joe wanted to interest someone with more capital into making the claims into a producing mine. The Quigleys hoped the new railroad would reduce transportation costs for supplies being shipped in and ore being shipped out: with an improved system of transportation, their ores might be economically developed.

The town of Nenana, once a simple Athabascan Indian fish camp and trading post on the Tanana River, was chosen by the new Railroad Corporation as a major headquarters for the Northern Region. Beginning with an auction of town lots in 1916, the railroad constructed offices, yards, shops, housing, and a hospital in Nenana. The new town even gained its own newspaper, the *Nenana News*. The paper was solidly in the camp of the town boosters, men who were pushing to see the place solidify and prosper, hopefully as the transshipment point for the mineral wealth that was the reason behind the development of the new railroad in the first place. Alaskans were always convinced that prosperity was just around the corner: if they only had decent, affordable transportation, then the mineral wealth they all knew was there could be profitably developed. The Quigleys' Kantishna ore properties of course fit right into this story line, so the news-

paper documented every step of the development process and every visit of the Quigleys to Nenana.

Joe and Fannie made a trip to the newly constructed town in February 1919, a trip that took three days. The *Nenana News* reporter noted that it was Joe's fourth and Fannie's third trip to an Alaskan town in the thirteen years she had been living in Kantishna: "Both Mr. and Mrs. Quigley were greatly struck with the appearance of the town of Nenana and its growth. Nenana was not much of a place as far as looks went, when they happened to be here on a previous occasion." The Quigleys made contacts for transportation and supplies, and Joe used the opportunity to get a toe amputated in the railroad hospital. After his recovery, the Quigleys returned to Kantishna via the partially completed railroad. Fannie took the train to the "Jap Roadhouse," named for its Japanese proprietor (its location was later designated Kobe, the present-day Rex), and Joe followed with the dog team.[11]

Perhaps Joe used the trip to finalize an important new deal, for later in 1919, he succeeded in leasing his Little Annie claims to Fairbanks mine operator Thomas Aitken. It was to be the first production of galena, a silver-lead ore, in the Kantishna District. Thomas Aitken had been actively mining silver back in the Yukon at Keno Hill, where his Silver King mine was one of the first in that area to be successfully developed. Fannie must have

Nenana early in its development as a railroad town. *ASL Skinner Foundation Collection PCA 44-6-99*

periodically heard reports of the tremendous silver boom in the Clear
Creek District and remembered her earlier experiences there. In fact, the
minerals on Quigley Ridge in the Kantishna were similar to those in the
Keno area. However, the Keno–Duncan Hill District, on the wide and navi-
gable Stewart River, a tributary of the Yukon, enjoyed the kind of transportation access that Kantishna would never be able to achieve. The first
stage road to the area from Dawson was constructed in 1902. By 1904, the
main stage route between Whitehorse and Dawson ran on the route of the
1900 stampeders. By the 1930s, photos show thousands of sacks of ore

waiting on the docks at Stewart and Mayo for riverboat shipment to the smelters.[12] Aitken used his experience to develop the Quigleys' Little Annie, a long-hoped-for milestone in the growth of the Kantishna.

Both the miners and the commercial interests in Nenana saw the Aitken lease as a watershed, signaling the start of large-scale commercial mining, the beginning of the bright future that they all saw so clearly. The *Nenana News* followed every move by Aitken and his crews and turned every report into an editorial. "The decision of Mr. Aitken to develop the Galena properties on a comprehensive scale marks the commencement of a new era for the Kantishna country, which has long awaited the coming of capital to put the properties on a producing basis," the editors opined in a typical story. "With one property producing, it is argued, it will not be difficult to secure backing for the many other propositions, which are awaiting development." As the *News* continued, " In fact, it is confidently believed by those familiar with Kantishna conditions that the district will soon be the scene of great activity, with an influx of people rivaling the stampede of earlier days, when thousands were attracted to the district by the discovery of rich placers."[13]

Aitken's plan for the Quigley claims involved establishing a transshipment point at Roosevelt on the Kantishna River. Freight and equipment for the mine would be shipped to Roosevelt by boat. From Roosevelt, longtime packer Ed Bartlett would haul the supplies 30 miles overland with horses to the mine, the first 8 miles on packhorses, then by buckboard for 14 miles before the supplies were transferred to a heavier wagon. The ore from the rich ledge on the Little Annie claim would be hauled back by Bartlett and his freighters to Roosevelt, where the sacks of ore would be stacked until spring to be shipped back down the Kantishna River, down the Yukon to St. Michael, and by ocean boats to the smelter in California. Undoubtedly, Aitken was hoping to use this as a test to develop a larger paying mine at the site, even though it seemed likely that with the repeated loading and unloading, only the most valuable ores would be profitable. In any event, problems developed almost immediately.

Aitken and his crew arrived in late May 1919 and headed up to Kantishna with boatloads of supplies, but the ground between Roosevelt and the mine was so boggy that even the packhorses could not get through, and wagons would only be able to be used in the winter. So all the supplies going to Roosevelt via the river would have to be landed before freeze-up, then held there until the snow fell before they could be transported to the mine. Needless to say, this added to the cost and complexity of developing the property. Then, things went from bad to worse: when river charterers

Packer Ed Bartlett's camp at Roosevelt on the Kantishna River, for the Aitken mining venture. *UAF Frederick B. Drane Collection 91-046-693*

Moore and Moody landed their final loads of supplies at the beginning of October, it was so late in the season that their boats were frozen in the ice of the Bearpaw River. The two men were compelled to leave the boats and hike cross-country to the railroad. They "siwashed it" for five days on the trail, the local jargon for the nights of impromptu camping without tents or even blankets.[14]

At the mine end, moving the ore down the steep hill from the portal to Moose Creek was described as the most serious problem—ultimately accomplished by rough-locked wagons, that is, wagons with their wheels chained to provide additional drag as they descended. Yet despite the setbacks, the supplies got through, and the first sacks of ore were stacked at Roosevelt at the beginning of December to wait for spring and shipment by riverboat. Bartlett was said to be hauling 7 tons of ore a day with his string of seventeen to twenty horses. By January, mining was in full swing, with fourteen or fifteen men working day and night. Although Aitken himself remained mum on the value of the claims, unofficial reports reaching the *Nenana News* described "a stringer of galena that runs from a few inches to three feet, that is said to run all through from $300 to $4,200 to the ton in silver, besides carrying gold from a few dollars to $160, and also two percent copper."[15] The *News* was, as usual, guilty of unbridled optimism, as

Fannie sawing wood. *UAF Fannie Quigley Photo Collection*

later reports confirmed values of only $170 to $200 per ton. Yet even the very fact that the ore was being carried by packhorse in an era when mining in other districts was already highly mechanized seemed to dampen no one's enthusiasm; if it did, they kept it to themselves for the time being. Unreported in the *News* was Fannie's part of the job: cooking for the crew as well as cutting the wood to keep four woodstoves going through the winter.

In all probability, Fannie and Joe made the final move to the site on the east end of Quigley Ridge that spring of 1919 as they finalized the deal with Aitken to work the claims there. The new cabin was sited on a flat bench dug into the hillside, high enough to get good sun and perhaps 100 feet above Friday Creek. This was to be Fannie's home for the next twenty years. The new cabin, frequently photographed, bears such a close resemblance to the cabin from the Silver Pick claim that it seems likely they actually moved it to the new site. Wood was so scarce and logs for cabins were in such short supply that disassembling and reassembling such buildings was common practice.

In April 1920, while Fannie and Joe and Aitken's crew were busy at the mine, the dreaded and deadly influenza epidemic that had decimated the rest of the world in the two previous years crept stealthily into Fairbanks and Nenana. The first cases were reported on April 27, and the disease spread rapidly, despite all precautions. Flu patients in Nenana were at first housed at the government hospital, but by May 3, with over two hundred cases in town, patients filled the hospital and the railroad dormitories and then took over the Cooney and Southern hotels. Railroad work came to a standstill, as patients were brought in over the line. As the epidemic progressed in both towns simultaneously, every available person was drafted for nursing duty. A call went out for more volunteers.[16] As the paper explained: "More nurses is the crying need of the hour in Nenana just at present to relieve those who have been taken ill and to look after the new cases that are coming in all of the time. Very few of the nurses who began work

The Quigley claims on the west end of Quigley Ridge under mining development as the Red Top Mine. Pictured are the Quigley cabin, piles of firewood, a woodshed, a blacksmith shop, and a bunkhouse. The mine itself may have been accessed by a tunnel, covered by the tent, up the hill from the other structures. *UAF John Brooks Collection 68-32-324*

when the epidemic started are on the job now, and it has been no small task to find volunteers to take their places and to assist in the new work that has developed in connection with the opening of additional emergency hospitals."[17] By May 5, the tone was more desperate still, with a headline urging: "NENANA MUST HAVE MORE NURSES NOW."

The photo I always found the most puzzling in the Fannie Quigley Collection at the University of Alaska Archives shows her in front of a large building in a group photo as part of a medical staff.[18] She is recognizable as the most petite person in the picture. It was easy to assume that this was a hospital, but for years, I wondered where this hospital might have been. Was it somewhere on the Union Pacific line, perhaps in Wyoming or at Portland or Seattle? Eventually, I came across a photo of the Alaska Railroad Hospital in Nenana that matched perfectly. For some reason, even after years in Alaska, I had never realized that the railroad buildings in Nenana were constructed on such a large scale. Abandoned just a few years after the buildings were completed, the entire complex later burned down. Then, in the 1960s, when the state of Alaska built the Parks Highway, the new bridge approach cut directly through the site. And today, the village of small cabins affords no hint of its former administrative scale. Even after I matched

Fannie is the smallest person in this photo with a group in front of the Alaska Railroad Hospital, Nenana. *UAF Fannie Quigley Photo Collection 80-46-222*

The Alaska Railroad Hospital at Nenana. The wide porch to the left is where the hospital staff posed for the previous photo. *UAF Albert J. Johnson Collection 89-166*

the photo with others of the railroad hospital, I was left to wonder why Fannie was in the photo. I can only assume that she was responding to the devastating flu epidemic. Word must have reached her in Kantishna, prompting her to make the trip into Nenana to volunteer.

By May 14, the epidemic had nearly run its course, and the last of the patients were moved from the Southern Hotel back to the hospital. The epidemic decimated the Native population in Nenana Village and surrounding camps. Twenty-seven deaths were reported in the village, with five dead at Totchaket, four at Wood River, and several more at the Native village near Chena.[19]

Just how bad the transportation problem was in Kantishna was amply demonstrated when, after a long winter of mining and freighting, the *Reliance,* a small boat with a shallow draft, began to haul Aitken's ore from Roosevelt to the mouth of the Kantishna in June 1920. The boat made two trips hauling 333 tons, but low water and big sandbars impeded progress, and the boat was forced to wait for rain to raise the river level. It became all the more apparent that only the highest-quality ores were worth shipping down the rivers and on the circuitous route to the smelter in Selby, California. The Quigleys were said to have received $10,000 for their property, in addition to which Aitken was to pay them something over

$200,000 as the ore was taken from the ledges.[20] The conclusion that Aitken would high-grade the claim—mine only the richest ores and pull out—was nearly inescapable.

The failure of the *Reliance* to move Aitken's ore nearly doomed mining in the Kantishna. But the many difficulties of transportation, together with the impending completion of the railroad, fired up the commercial interests in Nenana to try to solve the Kantishna's transportation problems. While constantly hoping that larger and richer mineral discoveries would force the issue of transportation, town boosters simultaneously worked to obtain government funding for a road or railroad to make the mines already working economical. At the very least, they hoped to get government funds to improve the existing trails.

On July 19, an optimistic Lt. Col. John Gotwals of the Alaska Road Commission (ARC) arrived in Nenana and announced: "You can tell the people of the Kantishna district, Nenana and all other interested sections that immediate steps will be taken by the Alaska Road Commission to put the Roosevelt–Moose Creek wagon road in the Kantishna in condition for traffic, and that the Road Commission will undertake repair work on the Roosevelt road with funds on hand." Gotwals, an experienced army man, believed that the time had come for the commission to construct roads for the use of trucks—"feeder highways," he called them—which would serve both the railroad and the interior waterways. The colonel was a firm believer in the value of truck roads, having witnessed their efficacy during the war in France, as the Nenana reporter explained: "It had been demonstrated the supplies could be moved more cheaply and quickly over short distances by truck than by railroad, through elimination of handling at each end of the haul. And he believes truck roads are the great need of the country, connecting with the Government trunk line railroad and with the various rivers."[21]

This pipe dream played well to the Nenana Commercial Club. But, of course, it was an impossibility until ample funds could be secured. Gotwals was hoping for appropriations of $1 million a year, which was wildly optimistic. The whole episode was really just a big buildup for the Alaska Road Commission's efforts to simply improve the sorry condition of Bartlett's pack-trail through the swamps from Roosevelt to the Quigleys' mines. In late July, George Black's steamer the *Pioneer* arrived from Fairbanks with the ARC road-building crew and a cargo of supplies and men for Roosevelt, with plans to "corduroy" (lay a wood roadbed) the first 8 swampy miles of the road.

The corduroy road. The Alaska Road Commission in 1921 used logs laid down side by side across the muddy bogs to improve Bartlett's trail for the Aitken Mine.
UAF John Brooks Collection 68-32-314

Meanwhile, Andy Livingston's power boat *Kestrel* was pressed into service to try to haul the remainder of the Aitken ore. With the river now full to the banks at Roosevelt and much of the surrounding country inundated because of recent heavy rains, Livingston succeeded in delivering two loads of ore to the mouth of the Kantishna, and he expected to haul the remainder in one more load. In spite of the difficulties with transporting the ore, Aitken announced plans to employ fifteen men to mine over the 1920–21 winter. And meanwhile, the population in the district was climbing to over one hundred.[22]

Then suddenly, in February 1921, Aitken announced that he was pulling out. As the *Nenana News* explained it, he "tried to get possession of a very rich ledge which Quigley is now developing, but it is claimed that he was not successful and therefore was going to quit the district, forfeiting his equity in the properties."[23] Joe Quigley's rich ledge was on the Red Top Lode, adjoining the Aitken group on the west. Having exposed the ore body, showing more galena, throughout 1921, Joe worked on a 40-foot shaft and a 200–foot drift following the vein. When the geologists came to inquire about the abrupt end to the Aitken deal, Joe cited the 200 ounces per ton that Aitken had averaged in 1919 versus the 170 ounces per ton in 1920, and he accused Aitken of careless mining.[24] But mining is like poker, and either side could have made up or enhanced a story simply to get out of the deal.

Meanwhile, Fannie, as part owner of the claims, had undoubtedly been hoping that the Aitken deal was the big sellout she had been working for. She must have often pictured Aitken making his final payment in December 1922, finally enabling them to leave as successes. But as the fall of 1920 turned into winter and 1921 began, she must have gradually realized that her husband was convincing himself that they would be better off mining the property themselves. For Fannie and Joe, the work was only beginning when Aitken walked off the property.

Joe was vindicated in September 1922 when he successfully leased his new discovery, the Red Top, to Hawley Sterling, a local Fairbanks man who was later to work for the ARC on the Park Road. Sterling mined the high-grade ore near the mine portal, taking out approximately 50 tons, which was hauled by dog team to Kobe and shipped via the new railroad to Seward and then on to the smelter in Tacoma. Another 102 tons of ore were mined in 1923. Meanwhile, Quigley had extended the workings to 500 feet of tunnel, with drifts and shaft and a main adit extending more than 300 feet. According to government geologists, the Red Top claim produced a

Joe, the businessman *(on left)*, sent this photo postcard to Fannie while they were on their one trip outside Alaska, but apparently in different cities, November 1923. "Will be here a few days, yet." The other figure in the photo is unknown. *NPS-DENA*

total of 184 tons of ore between 1922 and 1923, yielding 43,664 ounces of silver, 187 ounces of gold, and 93,200 pounds of lead.[25]

While all this was going on, it is likely that Joe was mining and shipping some ore on his own account, as Fannie indicated in a letter to her sister: "Joe made up his mind to ship some ore this winter that is only time we can ship is in winter."[26] And Fannie's efforts were essential to keeping the operation going, cutting and hauling wood for the house, bunkhouse, and blacksmith shop and undoubtedly cooking for the crew. "We been having very bad weather last summer rain winds and this winter snow and wind. I hope it will let up soon it takes so much wood when wind is blowing we have to pay 22 for cord we have 4 stoves going 2 in house and 1 in bunkhouse 1 in blaks shop. I do all cutting wood that is only way I can keepe fat down."[27]

For Fannie, it was yet more unrelenting hard work, and although she tried to put things in a positive light, as a way to "keepe fat down," she still expressed the hope that she would be able to take a trip "outside" to visit. Joe and Fannie finally made that trip in the fall and winter between 1923 and 1924. It was Fannie's only trip to the States in her entire sojourn in the North, a trip cataloged in photographs. Ruth Carson, a relative of Joe's, wrote of that visit, "Fannie was a warm, wonderful person recounting almost unbelievable stories of adventure in her Alaska which she loved dearly and emphatically."[28]

Wilderness Life
Cooking and Gardening

FANNIE GAINED HER FIRST AND GREATEST NOTICE as a wilderness cook. The young artist and adventurer Belmore Browne and his climbing party were especially grateful when they encountered her on their return from an attempted climb of Mount McKinley in 1912. And in his 1913 *Outing Magazine* article, Browne wrote the first testament in print to Fannie's wilderness cooking: "First came spiced, corned moose-meat, followed by moose muffle jelly. Several varieties of jelly made from native berries covered the large slices of yeast bread, but what interested me more was rhubarb sauce made from the wild rhubarb of that region. . . . These delicacies were washed down with great bowls of potato beer, ice-cold from the underground cellar."[1] This description illustrates the range of ingredients that could go into one meal, from the home-processed wild game to produce from the garden and the wild rhubarb and berries that Fannie picked by the gallon to make jams and jellies. And of course, the potato beer was another homestead product: with Fannie's affinity for alcohol, she always had some kind of home product available.

Cooking, gardening, and putting up food were apparently never far from Fannie's thoughts; indeed, she talked about these tasks in nearly every letter she wrote. "I have all kines of berrys" was among the first things she reported in one of her earliest letters to her sister, mailed in August 1907. In 1913, she wrote, "I am putting up meat for summer and starting up plants. I wish that you could see the lettuce, cauliflower and celery." And in 1923, she noted, "I did not have much of garden I wish that you could see Celery and Cauliflower. I head good Strawberry and rhubarb. I take half and half for pie that some pie."[2]

In many ways, Fannie made use of the traditional, Old World techniques and skills she had learned as a girl growing up on the Bohemian homestead in Nebraska. She grew as much of what was needed as possible, put up and preserved food, and made do and did without. Fannie's cooking skills were legendary, but in addition to her abilities as a chef, her fine meals depended on four main activities: hunting for wild game, gardening, gathering wild foods, and preserving food. For her admirers, those who had had the opportunity to meet her and sample her cooking, the miracle was the size and quality of her meals and the variety of foods she managed to produce in such a remote location.

As Grant Pearson related, "I once had a Christmas dinner with Fannie that consisted of black bear roast, gravy, mashed potatoes, fresh cabbage, hot rolls, currant jelly, cranberry sauce, and blueberry shortcake. Only the flour and sugar had been freighted in, the rest was off the country."[3] Because everything that Joe and Fannie could not grow, catch, gather, or hunt had to be purchased for cash and hauled in over 100 miles by a dog team, usually a year's worth at a time, Fannie's efforts were extremely valuable to the mining enterprise that was the focus of the Quigleys' activities. And Fannie was well aware of this value, as she frequently reminded visitors. In that regard, Fairbanks attorney Tom Marquam experienced her wrath and biting humor on a visit to Kantishna. According to Grant Pearson, after Fannie brought in dessert after serving Marquam dinner, she noticed a piece of butter left on her guest's plate: "You eat that butter or you'll get the same plate with the butter still on it for breakfast!" she announced.[4] And she said much the same thing to Lois McGarvey, a neophyte trapper who visited in the early 1920s. Fannie served her a wonderful dinner, "Caribou chops cut thick, English style, and cooked to a king's taste!" But Lois had to confess to Fannie that she could not stomach the two inches of fat all around the chops. "Oh that's all right," Fannie replied, "I'll just fry it over for your breakfast."[5]

Fannie's first garden in the Kantishna was on Glacier Creek, just where the creek emerges from the narrow valley and the steep hills. There, on the high bench overlooking the creek at claim No. 14 Above, where Joe had first built his cabin, Fannie had settled in. After filing on claims during the winter, she put in her first Kantishna garden in the summer of 1907. Belmore Browne and his companions arrived there at the end of their 1912 expedition after hiking overland from the base of Mount McKinley to the

Kantishna River. Their first stop was on Moose Creek, probably at the present site of the Kantishna townsite. From that point, Browne said, they followed Moose Creek for a few miles before heading east over rolling hills (the flanks of Wickersham Dome). "On the height of land between Moose and Glacier Creek we rested," he wrote, "and as we descended the last slope we saw an American flag waving on a thin flagpole. Then the roof of a cabin came into view, and we were soon welcomed into the palatial home of Fannie McKenzie." Of course, the home that seemed "palatial" to Browne, though bigger than the average one-room prospector's cabin, was still probably no more than a 16-foot-by-20-foot cabin. "Through the window" Browne wrote, "you could see a flower garden, while below the cabin a truck garden flourished inside a pole fence." Browne called Fannie "one of the most remarkable women I have ever met" and gave a vivid description of her, noting that she was called "Mother McKenzie" by the miners from Moose Creek to Tolovana. "Of medium height, her body had the strength and ruggedness of a man's. Below her short skirt came the leather of her rubber shoe packs and a flannel shirt covered her strong shoulders. But the most striking part of her were her keen, humorous eyes."[6]

Over the next five years, Fannie developed the gardening techniques that she would go on to perfect during the rest of her life in the Kantishna. Her tenacity, energy, and green thumb were readily apparent to mining geologist Stephen Capps, who visited her in 1915. Capps documented her extensive garden, recognizing the critical economic value of subsistence activities to mining development. A photo he took shows that Fannie had built an enclosed garden, with two raised beds along the perimeter beside the cabin. She had erected a superstructure over the bed up against the side of the cabin, which could have functioned as a cold frame; though she had no plastic or glass, she could at least cover the bed with canvas at night to protect the plants. She undoubtedly hauled up the fine dirt from the creek bed there, as she later did on Friday Creek. Developing the soil in raised beds allowed her to concentrate her efforts in as small an area as possible. Some photos show an impromptu greenhouse, as well, which she must have set up in the spring. Down by the creek, she cultivated a second garden site inside a pole fence.[7]

Noting that an elevation of 1,900 feet and a location above tree line was an exceedingly difficult environment for growing things, Capps described the garden in detail: "This year by Aug. 1 on Fannie McKenzie's garden cauliflower was matured, cabbages well grown, but barely beginning to head, lettuce in great heads, radishes over mature, onions mature, new

The garden at Glacier Creek, in raised beds to the side of the cabin. Note the support structure for covering the beds. *UAF Stephen R. Capps Collection 83-149-1867*

potatoes 2½" in diameter. Rhubarb, rutabagas, cucumbers grow well. Certain varieties of tomato ripen." Fannie also cultivated strawberries: "Five big strawberry plants in garden, but no berries, (plants second year)." And she had flowers: "Gardens of flowers (poppies of several varieties) bloom in late July. Pansies and many beautiful wild flowers of wide variety including wild yellow poppies."[8]

In addition to the garden vegetables, Fannie harvested local grasses for hay that was used to bed the dogs. As Capps noted, "Volunteer timothy matures in July. Oats ripen well." She also utilized another garden site on Bear Creek to grow corn, as he reported: "Corn was well-filled in their ear at fish camp by early July." Capps ranged widely over the hills during his stay, investigating and describing mining operations and sketching the tunnels and workings, but he stayed camped at Quigley's, sometimes referred to as "Quigley-McKenzie." Where else could he be assured of such good meals?[9]

Fannie and Joe gradually moved their mining operations to Quigley Ridge, beginning as early as 1913, as Joe developed some of his hard rock mining claims. But they returned to Glacier Creek in the summers, where Fannie continued her gardening. In her 1913 letter to her old friend Charles Sheldon, she was still talking about gardening. "I am putting up meat for summer and starting up plants. I wish that you could see the lettuce, cauliflower and celery. Every man has a garden in this camp."[10] As Fannie

The garden at Friday Creek on Quigley Ridge, ca. 1923. *UAF Stephen R. Capps Collection 83-149-23*

and Joe came to place their hopes in Joe's Little Annie and Red Top claims on the north and west sides of Quigley Ridge, overlooking Moose Creek, they also moved their cabin and center of activity. By 1919, when they leased the claims to Tom Aitken, they had consolidated their activities on the site where Fannie would be frequently pictured in photographs from the 1920s and 1930s, often showing off her garden to visitors.

After the move, Fannie began developing her terraced hillside garden. Today, from the road to the Moose Creek Airstrip in Kantishna, if you look up at the hillside, what you see is a patch of poplar trees. I had visited Kantishna more than a few times looking for the remains of her cabin before I figured out that the patch of trees *is* Fannie's garden. The carefully constructed terraces, with the dirt hauled up basket by basket, are the only soil on the hillside and thus the only site that can support trees. The stone retaining walls both terraced the hillside and warmed the dirt early in the spring, and a stout chicken-wire fence protected the garden and each bed. Climbing up the steep hillside among the trees, one can still find the remains of the stone terraces and the chicken wire underneath decades of thick moss. Higher up the hillside, on a small flat space at the top of the garden, are the remains of the stone planting bed surrounding the cabin, in which Fannie grew flowers and sometimes even corn. "I have good garden—lettuce heads like cabbage—nice strawberries and so many all kinds berries," she

said in a letter to Mary Lee Davis. And in a letter to her sister from the same
era, she noted, "We ar having a bad winter and we head bad summer no rain
and poor garden we head good Cabbage and tomatos that was about all."[11]

  Wild game was a central feature of Fannie's cooking, and later in her
life, she became famous as a hunter herself, so I was surprised to discover in
her first letter to her sister, mailed in August 1907, that she had never killed

Above: Corn growing in the foundation boxes at Fannie's cabin on Friday Creek. *UAF Fannie Quigley Photo Collection 80-46-273. Below:* Vegetables and flowers in Fannie's garden. *UAF Fannie Quigley Photo Collection 80-46-278*

an animal before arriving in the Kantishna country: "You see I left Chena year ago last august. I am close to Mount McKinley only 15 miles. Well I kill big moose this fall first thing that I ever kill in my life. He waid 800 pounds dress." Caribou and moose were the mainstays of the wilderness diet, but in the McKinley area, the Quigleys could often get sheep as well. And they must have eaten their share of rabbits and the ptarmigan, which are similar to quail. Later, Fannie's prowess at hunting added not only to her fine meals but to her growing reputation as a wilderness woman. She wrote Mary Lee Davis about her gardening, hunting, and hard work during the time that Joe was in the hospital in the summer of 1930: "I got big moose, dresses about eight hundred pounds. It was very fat. And some good fat caribou—one white like sheep. . . . Went down six miles to-day for some meat I killed. Then I have about fifteen cords wood to haul, so you see when night comes I am tired."[12]

The third cornerstone of Fannie's food supplies was wild foods—cranberries, blueberries, and wild rhubarb. Blueberry pie was a staple, and for Belmore Browne, she prepared "rhubarb sauce made from the

Fannie with her rhubarb.
UAF Fannie Quigley Photo Collection 80-46-209

Fannie Quigley's Blueberry Pie

First, in early August pick five gallons of blueberries as they ripen on the hillside in back of your mining claim.

Before the creeks run dry in the summer, pan some gold out of your claim.

Then, in early fall, shoot a good fat bear. Skin the bear, and butcher it. Haul it, one quarter at a time, in your backpack, to your cabin.

When the first snows come to the hills, hitch up the dogs and mush fifteen miles down the valley for firewood. Haul ten or fifteen cords to keep the woodstove going in the cabin for the winter.

Using a large iron kettle and the wood you've hauled, render the bear fat into lard.

Hitch up the dogs again, and mush 125 miles to Nenana. Trade some of your gold dust for 100 pounds of flour and 50 pounds of sugar. Load it onto your sled and mush home. Be sure to avoid the overflow on the Toklat River so the flour doesn't get wet.

Use the bear fat lard and the flour to bake a dozen flaky pie crusts in the oven of your wood cookstove. Keep the stove stoked with good dry wood to maintain a high temperature.

Mix the blueberries with some sugar, and add enough flour to bind up the juices. Put the filling into the crusts and bake. Don't let the fire in the stove get too hot, or the pies will burn.

Cool the pies, then store them frozen in the permafrost mining tunnel behind the cabin.

When company comes, go out and get a pie out of the tunnel. It will taste as good as fresh and astonish your guests.

Jane G. Haigh

Another shot of Fannie with rhubarb. By this point Joe had taken up photography, leaving many informal and candid shots of the Quigleys' life in the Kantishna. *UAF Fannie Quigley Photo Collection 1980-0046 00509*

wild rhubarb of that region." Preserving and processing the produce, meat, and berries was as important as the hunting, growing, and gathering. Browne observed Fannie's first attempts at cold storage in 1912: "To the east was a large, well-stocked underground cellar, where even in summer time a bucket of water placed on the floor would freeze." And Stephen Capps reported in 1916, "Potatoes are varied in quantity and they and lettuce, cabbage, cauliflower, turnips, rutabagas, and fine celery can be stored for winter use."[13]

While Joe mined, Fannie hooked up the dogs and took the sleds down to the timber on Moose Creek and cut trees for firewood, then hauled the wood back in long lengths with the dogs. Then, back at the mine, she cut the logs into stove lengths for exercise, as she once wrote her sister. By 1921, when Mary Lee Davis visited her, Fannie had been settled on Friday Creek for two or three years. According to Mary Lee, Fannie and Joe hunted in the fall and kept the meat in the back of Joe's mining tunnels, along with the root crops from the garden and the cabbages, berries, or apples that they had sent in. Sometimes, Fannie told Mary Lee, she salted down the meat or cooked it and then froze it in the back of the tunnels. The system of tunnels was well developed by 1933, when mining engineer Ira Joralemon visited with mining investor General A.D. McRae, who later optioned the property. "Fanny's root cellar was really a short tunnel in the gravel bank behind her house," Joralemon reported, "connected with the back door of the kitchen

by a 10-ft. walkway covered with split pine shakes. Even in the coldest weather she could go to the root tunnel without freezing."[14] Although Jo-ralemon described a root cellar elaborately connected to the house, no such cellar has yet been found. (And of course, there were no pine shakes in the vicinity).

Fannie seems to have used many of her Bohemian homestead skills in preserving meat and preparing traditional products designed to use the whole animal. *The Bohemian Cookbook*, originally published in 1949, in-cluded many such traditional recipes compiled from the immigrants in Ne-braska. For instance, the "spiced corned moose meat, followed by moose muffle jelly" that Fannie served Belmore Browne "could have been made from a Bohemian corned beef recipe in the cookbook:

> For 200 pounds meat take six or seven pounds of salt and one box of ground assorted spices. Two heads of garlic mashed to a paste with salt may also be added. Mix all together and rub over the meat. The meat is then packed into a jar or keg, so that there are no crevices between the pieces. Place a board or weight on top."[15]

Likewise, the moose muffle jelly was a variation of headcheese, com-monly made with pork:

Fannie in front of her main cabin at the west end of Quigley Ridge, near Friday Creek. By this time the cabin had stone-enclosed planting beds around the foundation, where they would absorb and hold heat from the sun. *UAF Fannie Quigley Collection 80-46-220*

Boil pork from the leg, the head, the ears, snout and tongue. When done, trim out the bones, cartilage, etc, skin the tongue, cut all into small pieces. Have ready a round form, such as a bucket. In the bottom place a layer of meat from the leg, dust with salt, pepper, mace, then put in a layer of the ears and snout, dust with salt, etc. then a layer of the tongue, and continue until the dish is full. Cover, place a weight on top, and let stand in a cool place overnight.[16]

Fannie might also have prepared "stuffed roast hare," "saddle of caribou with pepper sauce," or "stewed quail." The *Bohemian Cookbook* even included a recipe for bear steak, "*Medvedi kyta*."[17]

Fannie relied on imported items only to complement the food she grew and prepared herself. The eggs she used were shipped in by the cask, once a year: as she wrote one of her sisters, "We got cask of eggs they com from Anacortes every time I bake one I say maybe this is one Marys hen lade."[18]

The sum of all these processes, ingredients, and efforts was the complete meal, like the one she served Grant Pearson when he first met her in 1926 as a young park ranger. It featured caribou steak, potatoes, beets, carrots, and rhubarb from her own garden, together with blueberry pie with a flaky crust made from rendered bear fat. Grant learned many of his wilderness life skills from her—freezing and preserving food. She even harvested the wild hay and grasses, which she generously put out for visiting dogs. When Pearson thanked her, he claims she retorted, "It ain't for you bums of rangers I do this, its for the dogs!"[19]

Lois McGarvey provided the most complete account of daily life with Fannie, as she prepared for a few days on the trapline trail. She reported that Fannie spent a whole day cooking ahead—"a wonderful haunch of mountain sheep, juicy and tender, roasted to a turn; a flour sack full of donuts fried in bear fat, and awfully good, and frozen cranberries." Once out on the trail, oatmeal, bacon, and sourdough hotcakes was the normal fare, cooked on a small Yukon stove. Other meals Lois enjoyed courtesy of Fannie included mountain sheep steak and sheep chops.[20]

Virgil Burford was a young man in the waning days of World War II when he decided to do some prospecting in Kantishna. He would be one of the last people to visit Fannie and describe her home, including the corner of the room that functioned as the kitchen where she prepared her culinary miracles. He wrote, "The kitchen was small, most of one side was taken up by the plank table at which we sat. In a corner across the room there was a small porcelain sink with a drain through the plank floor. Gold pans sat about on the walls, half full of ore samples. A Yukon stove crouched against a far wall, throwing out a blaze of heat on this warm day." As Burford described it, the kitchen and its accoutrements took second place in the cabin to the evidence of mining activity: "One wall was lined with plank shelves, the shelves loaded with ore samples and rocks. A half dozen rusty pick heads were stacked in a corner with a small anvil and hammer."

Fannie served him in her inimitable style: "She brought out a loaf of homemade bread and a huge cold roast of caribou and a wedge of blueberry pie. 'Never saw a prospecting bum that wasn't starved,' she snapped. 'You eat that.'"[21]

She was still maintaining the garden, too, though perhaps by this time it was not as big as it had once been. Burford recalled:

> Outside I noticed her garden for the first time, It was small, built in neat terraces bordered with rocks. There were rhubarb, potatoes, radishes, lettuce, beets, celery and turnips. They all looked luscious and thriving. There was not a weed in sight. This garden had been cared for with loving hands and planted by someone with a very green thumb. I said "That's a fine garden. How do you get things to grow up here?"
>
> "Ain't it a dandy?" for the first time her small thin face broke into a smile.[22]

Fannie weeding her garden. Photo by Joe Quigley. *UAF Fannie Quigley Photo Collection 1980-0046-00501*

The Outdoor Life
Hunting and Trapping

> Well I kill big moose this fall first thing that I ever kill in my life.
> He waid 800 pounds dress.
>
> —Fannie Quigley, 1907

FANNIE WAS SO WELL KNOWN as a hunter and trapper by the 1930s that I was surprised to find out she had never hunted before she arrived in the Kantishna. I had imagined her learning to hunt back on the homestead in Nebraska, where small game was an important part of the Bohemian homesteaders' subsistence. But she was quite clear about this definitive beginning of her hunting career in the letter she sent to her sister in 1907.[1]

Since the late nineteenth century, the wilderness has been seen as a male preserve—a place to test and prove manliness—and hunting has always been an essential part of this test. Could a woman truly "penetrate virgin land" and "conquer the wilderness"? That Fannie did so was part of the paradox that sparked her many visitors to write about her as the quintessential wilderness woman.

Fannie had two excellent teachers in the earliest years in the Kantishna, Joe Quigley and noted big-game hunter Charles Sheldon. Sheldon described Joe as "one of those rare honest chivalrous men, . . . who combined successful individual mining with the traits of a true hunter and an accurate observer of Nature."[2] Fannie's education as a hunter began in earnest when she and Joe traveled out to Sheldon's remote cabin on the Toklat River to hunt sheep with him in early 1908. Of all the mammals one could hunt, perhaps the Dall sheep, in their habitat high up on the steep rock slopes, pose the greatest danger and demand the greatest skill on the part of the hunter. Sheldon, who was a close friend of Teddy Roosevelt and an active member of the Boone and Crockett Club, traveled to the Kantishna Mining District in the summer of 1906, just at the tail end of the two-year gold rush. He had hired young miner and dog musher Harry Karstens as camp man and guide to the habitat of the Dall sheep in the high valleys north of Mount McKinley. Sheldon was the epitome of the East Coast elite, a graduate of Yale who, by 1904 at the age of thirty-six, had attained independent wealth based on his successful investments in Mexican mining stocks during his service with the Chihuahua Railway in Mexico. A noted authority on mountain sheep, he was extolled in hunting circles as both a hunter and a naturalist and for his phenomenal physical strength and perseverance as well. Noted biologist C. Hart Merriam quoted George Bird Grinnell's description of him as "a splendid type of vigorous manhood, self-reliant, courageous." And as Merriam pointed out, Sheldon was not only a friend and fellow club member but also an exemplar for Roosevelt, who described him as "a capital representative of the best hunter-naturalist type of today."[3] Roosevelt was invoking the implicit connection recognized by the Boone and Crockett Club between big-game hunting and the new scientific interests represented by such organizations as the American Museum of Natural History and the Smithsonian Institution. Sheldon hoped to determine whether the different mountain sheep from Mexico through the Rockies to Alaska were members of the same family. Scientists need to compare specimens, and Sheldon's self-appointed job was to acquire those specimens, as well as to make observations on behavior and habitat. As Roosevelt explained, "He kept copious journals, and took meticulous notes on all manner of wildlife including birds, and mice, while collecting specimens of the larger game animals for the Biological Survey as well as for himself. His ability to write about his travels with an exciting vivacity drew others into his experiences."[4] That both Karstens and the Quigleys equally revered him is a testament to his fairness, lack of pretension, and unassuming tastes.[5]

On his short 1906 trip, Sheldon was so impressed with the area that he arranged to return and spend the 1907–8 winter studying the Dall sheep. Again, he hired Harry Karstens as guide, and they traveled up the Kantishna River. Low water forced the boat to stop, and they had to pack all of Sheldon's goods 20 miles more through mosquito-infested flats, then with packhorses up to the head of Glacier Creek, the point where the creek leaves the tight canyon in the hills and starts to meander through the vastness of the Kantishna Flats. This was where Sheldon, in his original journal, mentioned his first meeting with Fannie at Joe Quigley's property: "We reached Joe Quigley's at #15 Above and there passed the night. . . . Quigley is a hunter, and I enjoyed talking with him. . . . He has a woman living with him, 'Fanny' and a kind soul and rather interesting."[6]

At the end of February 1908, Joe and Fannie, already friends of Harry Karstens, traveled out to Sheldon's small cabin on the Toklat River to hunt. The cabin was no larger than 12 feet by 14 feet and already occupied by Sheldon and Karstens. That Fannie and Joe arrived with only three dogs indicates that they actually walked most or all of the 50 miles to the camp. Fannie was wearing a midcalf-length hooded canvas parka with a fur ruff over a long skirt and is pictured holding her 4-foot-long snow shoes.[7]

Of Sheldon's hunting technique, Merriam noted that "when hunting, he always hunted alone, well aware of the annoyance and failures attending the presence of a companion."[8] Amazingly, then, on two separate occasions during this two-week visit, Sheldon hunted with Fannie individually. These two days under the tutelage of a master hunter undoubtedly contributed to her growing skill. On February 22, Sheldon recorded: "On this day I went hunting with Mrs. Quigley [sic] and after an arduous mountain climb, which she made as easily as any man, we came close to a band of thirty four sheep. But her rifle missed fire twice, and then she missed them running."[9]

On February 23, the entire party headed up the Toklat River, where they again were able to observe sheep from the forks. Sheldon wrote, "Mrs. Quigley and I went a short distance up the Upper East Branch, where a band of rams was seen near the crest of the north end of Polychrome Mountain. After carefully studying the possible approaches we started a long and interesting stalk, once sitting still for an hour before we could move unseen." After the sheep went out of sight, they crept to within 150 yards: "After Mrs. Quigley's first shot they began to run upward and continued to run while she fired several times until they passed over the crest. None of the shots had taken effect and we returned to the cabin to find that the others also had been unsuccessful."[10]

Even though the hunt was ultimately unsuccessful, Fannie earned the respect of Sheldon, Karstens, and Quigley for the effort she made at sheep hunting in the high hills. She never forgot the lessons of close observation, careful and patient stalking, and using proper equipment.

If the two weeks of Sheldon's visit are a fascinating study, the three days between February 26 and 28, when they were all "confined to the cabin by a continuous heavy snow blizzard," beg for some creative interpretation. Unfortunately, though, all Sheldon offered was, "They had been delightful guests and I had greatly enjoyed their visit."[11]

Fannie never saw Sheldon again. On leaving his Toklat cabin in the spring, he did not return through Kantishna but instead traveled down the Toklat River. Nonetheless, he continued to stay in touch with Joe and Fannie. Clearly, they had learned much; their correspondence was frequently about wildlife, and over the years, Fannie and Joe each sent specimens to the Biological Survey, now a post of the Smithsonian Institution.

By the time Belmore Browne arrived four years later, in 1912, Fannie impressed him as an accomplished hunter and outdoorswoman, for this is how he described her: "She lived the wild life as the men did, and was as much at home in the open with a rifle as a city woman is on a city avenue, and she could not only follow and hunt successfully the wild game of the region, but could do a man's share in packing the meat to camp."[12]

Because many of Belmore's observations would be repeated time and again over the next thirty years until they became clichés, it is important to take a closer look, to analyze the texts in order to avoid falling into the trap of seeing Fannie as a stereotype. First, Browne acknowledged that living the wild life was a mostly masculine endeavor, as was the man's share in packing the meat to camp. In this sense, he began his masculinization of her as a character. Of more interest is Browne's observation or assumption that Fannie "was as much at home in the open with a rifle as a city woman is on a city avenue," a formulation that expressed volumes. In one telling phrase, he conveyed the rarity of a woman being at home in the wilderness, signaling her exceptionalism again and marking her difference from the seemingly average woman who was at home on a city street, and yet at the same time, he also managed to place Fannie "at home," that is, still within a domestic environment. If a woman's place was in the home, then Belmore (and others who followed him) expanded that idea, portraying all of nature as Fannie's pantry and locating her hunting and packing meat to camp in the domain of domestic responsibilities.[13] When Belmore described Fannie as an able fisherwoman, as happy as a boy, the fishing became as ordinary as a trip to the supermarket, and Fannie, though having a man's ability, is yet not quite a man. Fisherwomen were not unknown in the East, particularly in places such as the Adirondacks, and Belmore, only about thirty-two at the time, must have already encountered the young "new women" who, though outwardly conforming to class standards of dress and comportment, also took pleasure in wilderness and nature. Yet in describing Fannie as "a remarkable specimen of what a woman should be," Browne also described her as embodying masculine characteristics: "Of medium height, her body had the strength and ruggedness of a man's." Her dress was worthy of description because it differed so markedly from what would have been considered typical at the time: "Below her short skirt came the leather of her rubber shoe packs [heavy boots] and a flannel shirt covered her strong shoulders." The short skirt would have been seen as less than respectable, the strong shoulders were a masculine quality, and the flannel shirt and shoe packs were the typical prospector's attire. No wonder Belmore was confused! But if he was confused, it seems that the locals were not; they knew a woman when they saw one and were generally uninterested in predefining acceptable activity.

Phyllis Movius wrote about women in Alaska's interior, including Jesse Bloom, who moved to Fairbanks to join her husband in 1912. Movius was intrigued with Bloom's ideas about the role of women. As Movius observed, Jesse appreciated the different set of values and the idea that on the "less structured frontier . . . people did whatever needed doing regardless of preconceived gender roles." Having grown up in Ireland as a proper young upper-class woman and participated in suffrage demonstrations in London, Bloom felt that in the North, she was challenged to live a life "outside the bonds of conformity."[14]

Bloom herself may not have known Fannie, but a variety of other women visited her. Eager for a change of surroundings, young war widow Ruth Wilson of Omaha, Nebraska, made a trip to visit her brother, miner William Campbell, in Fairbanks in 1919. Then she accepted an invitation to join Fairbanks photographer Nan (Mrs. L. E.) Robertson on a trip into the Kantishna. Her adventures are documented in an article in the *Alaska Dispatch*, reprinted from the *Cordova Times*, and in many photographs. For the first leg of the trip, they traveled on a boat heading up the Kantishna River taking supplies to the Aitken mine. From Roosevelt, they hiked the 30 miles to Quigley Ridge "through the tangled and swampy wilderness, unmarked even by a trail." The highlight of the trip for Wilson was a chance to join Fannie and Joe Quigley "in their annual hunt to lay in the winter's meat." She herself shot a moose and a caribou. "Mrs. Quigley is a dead shot," she reported, "and has adapted herself perfectly to the lonely life." Ruth Wilson and Nan Robertson stayed in the area until December 1, "making their way out by dog team and frequently 'siwashing' under the open sky."[15]

Lois McGarvey traveled out to the Kantishna Mining District in the early 1920s to learn the art of trapping from Fannie. Lois had arrived in the interior as a single woman and spent a few years running a roadhouse outside Fairbanks prior to her marriage to a railroad engineer. Settled for a few years in Fairbanks, Lois was searching for a way to make money. She met Fannie through a friend in Fairbanks and then arranged transportation by dog sled out to Fannie's home. In her self-published memoir, Lois recounted her adventures and provided a window into Fannie's routine trapping operations in those years.[16]

Fannie *(left)*, Joe *(second from left)*, Joe Dalton *(right)*, and young widow Ruth Wilson, visiting the Kantishna on a fall hunting trip. *UAF Stephen Foster Collection 69-92-24*

Like other white miners and prospectors, Fannie was moving into the territory recently abandoned after the rural Athabascan population was decimated in the flu epidemic that reached the interior in 1920. The first days the women spent together were consumed with fixing up the string of trapping cabins on the 40-mile trapline. "There was a small sheet-iron Yukon stove in each shelter, a fry pan, a coffee pot, and a mush pot," Lois wrote. "We would have rolled oats for breakfast, with bacon and either sourdough hot cakes or bannocks." The conditions did not dissuade Lois, the prospective trapper who was determined to tough it out.

As her final test, Fannie assigned Lois to check the traps on one half of the trail:

> The next set was a lynx set; and as I came up there sat a great big beautiful cat, with the light gray silvery color that brought almost any price up to a hundred and fifty dollars! I got out my twenty-two pistol to shoot him in the head; but as I cautiously advanced, thinking he might pounce, he held up one paw, with the trap dangling and I saw he has been caught by one claw. Why the coward hadn't pulled loose before, even if it did hurt a little, I will never know. He continued to hold the paw up to me; and if a lynx can weep, he was weeping. I almost thought I saw tears. I sat on a log and looked at him a long time. So

simple to put the pistol and shoot, but so hard to with him looking right into my face. He was so pretty. I waited trying to get the butterflies out of my stomach, until I was nearly frozen stiff; then I reached out and got my end of the trap chain and gave a mighty jerk. Off came the lynx's toenail, and away went . . . my cash![17]

But the loss of the cash was not the end of it:

> At the same moment I felt a sinister presence. I looked nervously behind me, and there stood [Fannie] watching the lynx disappear. . . .
> "Now that is just enough of you! I knew something was screwy, as I gave you the best part of the line. You can just go to H__ back where you came from! You are a sissy and better go into a sissy business."

Lois McGarvey, the neophyte, was tough by any ordinary standards, but she was not nearly as tough as Fannie! In her memoir, she characterized herself as beset with anxieties related to typical female values: acknowledging butterflies in her stomach and empathy for the "big beautiful cat," even though she could calculate his monetary value. But it was Lois's characterization of Fannie's response that was particularly revealing. For Fannie, trapping was a business and a necessity; the wilderness was a productive environment, not a sentimental idyll.

After failing her test to become a trapper, McGarvey became a fur buyer, running her own dog team out to collect furs directly from the trappers. These extensive trips gave her a leg up on her competitors, who waited for the trappers to come to town at the end of the season. Lois herself could be considered a tough-as-nails Alaskan woman who challenged her environment and herself. Like Mary Lee Davis and Fannie, she seemed to have no preconceived ideas about limits on what women were able to do, but she found her own limits when she met Fannie.[18]

Mary Lee Davis was a Wellesley graduate, a former newspaper reporter, and an experienced surveyor who found herself living in Fairbanks as the wife of a mining engineer for the Bureau of Mines. She began writing books about Alaska to tell those "outside" about her newly adopted home. Together with her husband, on his way to make a survey of the mines, she traveled out to Kantishna to visit Fannie early in the 1920s over the proposed new trail through Mount McKinley National Park, a story she included in her book *We Are Alaskans*. They actually made the trip on horseback, a common mode of transportation for visitors at the time.[19]

Fannie showing off a lynx she has trapped. *Photo by Joe Quigley UAF Fannie Quigley Photo Collection 80-46-214*

When she finally reached the Kantishna cabin, where she spent a re-markable eleven days with Fannie, she was primed to listen to her hostess as a "Doctor of Nature Lore and Wilderness Living." Mary Lee continually made an effort to grant Fannie authority, by citing her friendship with great (male) hunters and explorers: "Fannie Quigley, my hostess for many days in the Kantishna is one of the real sports-women and all-around capable pi-oneers of the North. She has friends among the great hunters, explorers,

and scientists of all America, for her little Alaskan home on its steep mountainside has been a gathering place . . . of men intent on penetrating [!!] into
the farthest secrets of the hidden mountains.[20]

She described Fannie specifically as a huntswoman, delineating the skills
that she had acquired: "Not only a fine shot, and the peer of truly great
hunters, but tracks her own game, prefers to hunt alone, skins and dresses,
packs and caches even such massive beasts as moose and bear, skins out the
cape and horns of mountain sheep and can both butcher and cook any game
meat to the queen's taste."[21]

The heart of Davis's subject was Fannie's remarkable knowledge of
nature and natural history, evidence presented for that doctorate in nature
studies and wilderness living that Davis conferred on Fannie. After all, this
was a realm of scientific understanding already respected in the East. "The
hills are full of game. Even when you're stalking 'em they're really stalking you. I know that I've been watched—hunted, followed, tracked—by
bears and wolves, though never harmed. Afterward, when I've seen their
tracks in my old trails, it's made my back prickle. I've wondered just how
near they were."[22]

Mary Lee Davis presented Fannie the huntswoman as both interested
in and knowledgeable about nature and natural phenomena and connected
to and respected by other scientists. "And say, did I tell you what that fellow
from the Smithsonian was telling me—the one was here last summer what
I told you of?" In Mary Lee's representation, Fannie presented herself as
his equal: "We swapped a-plenty of such talk" but still in fact more capable;
she was even disdainful of his abilities, "Nice fellow, but weak legged, like
you." Fannie is both thoughtful and reflective, "I've thought of that a heap,"
yet common and uneducated, as indicated by her speech patterns.[23]

In her writing, Mary Lee highlighted the value of Fannie's domestic duties as an important component of her theoretical wilderness science degree: she marvels, "Consider the intelligence and foresight which must go
into ordering all one's groceries and mine supplies just once a year! That
is real shopping." Fannie's part of the domestic partnership included
everything from hunting, butchering, and storing meat to freighting supplies and firewood by dog team.[24] But Fannie's vision of her domestic duties, as expressed by Davis, extended beyond shopping. "Woman," Fannie
is quoted as saying, "Joe and I are pardners. His job is there, to work the
mine, and mine's the rest of it."[25] For Fannie, providing food was the para-
mount challenge.

Fannie took her hunting responsibilities seriously, and by the early
1920s, she was an expert. Mary Lee quoted Fannie as saying, "We take a

couple days off in the fall and can get all the caribou we want for a year's supply. Or moose or sheep."[26] She continued, "Quick death means clean butchering; and that counts, too, when you've got a carcass to handle alone, like I do. Heart, brains, or spinal cord is the mark. One well put bullet is enough—or should be! A shot in the gut means a messy job of butchering if you're out for meat. And a flank shot ruins a good hide if you're out for fur. YOU may be thinking of the mercy of it—that's open. I'M thinking about grubstake."[27]

But hunting and butchering were not the extent of Fannie's responsibilities. For storing food, she used Joe's mining tunnel, which was always below freezing: "Some meat I salt down. Some I cook and put away all sealed in its own fat and pile up in the tunnel, below freezing. Frost tenders it."[28]

Grant Pearson met Fannie when he was a young, green park ranger in the mid-1920s. He had been hired by Superintendent Harry Karstens, famous as one of the real Alaskan old-timers, but freely admitted that it was Fannie who taught him much of what he needed to know about living in the wilderness and traveling with dogs. By the 1950s, he had worked his way up to park superintendent. And it was Pearson who, in articles and a chapter in his ghostwritten autobiography, began and perpetuated many of the famous hunting stories involving Fannie.

Fannie was out to get her winter meat and managed to shoot a bull caribou right down by Moose Creek, below the cabin. But the big bull continued walking into a clump of willows, and Fannie assumed she had missed her shot. Right away, she saw a chance at another fat bull and took another shot. Then they both ran right into Moose Creek: "'The water was four feet deep and full of slush ice. When they got in the middle the darned fools fell dead; a nice fix to be in! Two caribou in the middle of a stream running with slush ice!'" Pearson continues the story as Fannie told it to him:

> "I came back and got some light rope, waded out and tied the rope to those two caribou. Then I tied the other end to a willow clump so when I got those critters free they wouldn't float downstream away from me. It took me at least an hour of tuggin' and luggin' to get 'em out, but I have all the caribou I'll need this winter."[29]

Pearson says he asked her if he could help butcher and cache the meat; she was said to reply, "Oh that's all done, you take it easy, dinner'll be ready soon."[30]

"I shall always remember my 'Most Unforgettable Character,'" Pearson wrote in another story about Fannie, and in fact, many of his stories put her in that very category—unforgettable, like the subject of a tall tale told

Fannie's dogs. Fannie relied on her dogs for her hunting and trapping trips and was famous for taking great care of them. *UAF Fannie Quigley Photo Collection 80-46-296*

by a couple of sourdoughs on a winter's night in front of the fire. It seems difficult to believe that Fannie had butchered and, most of all, made the trips to her cache with probably 300 pounds of meat before dark on a fall day with fading light. So, though probably based on the facts of Fannie being an expert at all things, I think the story is probably somewhat exaggerated.

Pearson told another story about Fannie, this one involving a wolverine. Wolverines are notoriously secretive yet dangerous and predatory; trapping one is the sign of a true professional. Pearson happened to stop at the Quigley cabin for a visit and found Joe in but Fannie still out on her rounds checking her trapline. Just about dark, she came back with her dog team and told the two men about finding one of her fox traps robbed by a wolverine. Knowing that if she did not catch the wolverine, he would continue to raid her traps, she told the two men, "I put out some traps for that so-and-so," at the same time reaching in and dragging the wolverine from her bag, "and here he is."[31]

Mary Lee Davis included another famous tale, the "wrapped in the bear skin" story, in her chapter about Fannie in *We Are Alaskans*:

> "Once I got lost, and had to take to clawing blueberries from the bushes like a bear. And once I shot a grizzly, 'long near dark, and when I got him skinned out, 'long came snow and it was too far off to make it into camp that night anyhow. So I think 'Well old bear, this thick hide kept

you warm a-plenty several years. Guess it can keep me warm one night.' So I wrapped up in it—warm yet, just skinned, you know—and slept sound. When I got in next morning my own dogs nearly ate me up! I was all bear grease and blood, head to foot, from that fresh hide. Looked pretty tough. Say, the pups never did get over smelling me! Good joke on them. Joe don't like to have me tell about that night, thinks it wasn't ladylike! Shucks—I wasn't aiming to sleep ladylike. I was hunting."[32]

Fannie hiking with her dogs, each with dog packs to help with the packing. *UAF 91-046-703 Frederick Drane Album #2*

Mary Lee Davis told this story in Fannie's words, as she did the many other hunting stories in her book. The complication is that this story is an apocryphal one told about many another character in Alaska as well. Whether or not it was true in Fannie's case, it becomes, in context, a story we think *could* be true and one that illustrates just how tough Fannie was as a hunter and how little interested she was in being ladylike. But if it is not true, why did Mary Lee Davis include it in her chapter and use Fannie's words and dialect as if Fannie had actually told it to Mary Lee herself? On the one hand, this certainly causes us to question the veracity of the rest of the stories set in Fannie's words; on the other hand, I think it inculcates the proper perspective—these are, in fact, all stories meant by Davis to convey ideas about Fannie. Her use of first-person dialect was, then, just a literary device.

In the winter of 1928, Fannie wrote to her sister and nephews that Joe had been working quartz all winter but added they were not going to ship ore that winter because they had lost money on the previous shipments due to high freight rates. Apparently, Fannie's hunting and trapping made up the difference in maintaining their subsistence existence. "Well boys [addressing her nephews] I been trapping and hauling wood I hauled 7 cords and got 5 fox 1 cross and 4 red and 2 lynx. I only got 6 trapps and I kill balck bear last fall and 4 caribou so you see keep me going we may get out next fall I hope so."[33]

Fannie kept on hunting until the end of her days. As described in Pearson's story about the two caribou, she could actually hunt right in the Moose Creek valley, just below her cabin, so she was still able to offer wandering prospector Virgil Burford a meal including a caribou roast just a few years before her death, when she was surely past seventy.

NINE

Wilderness Visitors

TO HER VISITORS, Fannie was a conundrum. Although she was notorious for her abrupt treatment and frequent swearing, she nonetheless presented a happy face to them, which they universally interpreted as "happier here in the wilderness than a city woman on a city street." (Meanwhile, of course, in letters to her family and friends, she complained about the endless work and the isolation she experienced as she dreamed of selling out.) At the core of Fannie's story is the simple fact she would not have been famous if she had not attracted so many visitors. To be sure, her life in the heart of Alaska was appealing, inspiring, and almost unimaginable, but the attention she received was mostly due to her location and proximity to the new national park. Visitors to the park naturally saw Fannie in relation to the wilderness. Since Teddy Roosevelt's adventures in the West in the late nineteenth century, the wilderness had been seen as a male domain, the ultimate proving ground for manliness. And almost all visitors to the park were pursuing their own romanticized vision of wilderness as something untamed. Consequently, Fannie and the domestic environment she was creating struck visitors as first of all surprising and then remarkable.[1]

But it is also true that the wilderness and Fannie attracted visitors, in particular Belmore Browne and Charles Sheldon, even before the establishment of the Mount McKinley National Park. Historian Roderick Nash recognized that there might be a difference in perception between Alaska locals and non-Alaskans in this regard. Non-Alaskans, beginning with John Muir in 1879, characterized Alaska's wilderness as "pure," "absolute," and "ultimate"; descriptors such as "nameless," "trackless," and "unknown" figured repeatedly in descriptive prose.[2]

Fannie's visitors all admired her for her wilderness skills, her determination, and the energy with which she confronted every task. But even though many observers would try to portray her as a symbol of the romantic wilderness, she herself lived entirely outside that romantic ideology in a wilderness lifestyle that was devoted to productive and often heartbreakingly hard work. Historian Richard White has reminded us that work is the means through which humans have traditionally learned about nature. Yet in our veneration of wilderness as an environment to escape from our civilized world and pursue recreational activities, we have, according to White, left work out.[3] For Fannie, work and wilderness were nearly synonymous, as she herself suggested in a letter to her niece in 1929: "Will Teresa there is no news here but worke."[4] Fannie was a survivor whose life began in a time when work and nature went together and ended in a time when wilderness was conceived as a space for leisure and the contemplation of nature as spectacle.

In the nature and adventure writing of the period, Alaska was portrayed as a qualitatively wilder wilderness. Its position was perceived as so far from center stage as to put it in a category of its own: an anomalous wilderness, a representation that author Susan Kollin has described as exceptionalism.[5] In her extended narrative examining nature writing about Alaska, Kollin argued that this writing "is still associated with male figures such as John Muir and Jack London" and that "nature and adventure writing in general are shaped by a master narrative involving an American Adam and his strategy of return to the wild." She describes Alaska as a space that "typically excludes or marginalizes female experiences."[6] In fact, in many accounts, Fannie herself was presented as exceptional, as a metaphor for Alaska: exotic, anomalous, outside of ordinarily understandable experience.

Ideas of wilderness as a male space and the confrontation with wilderness as a masculinizing endeavor were especially dominant in the early wilderness period, when Charles Sheldon and then Belmore Browne, the first two visitors to write about Fannie, arrived in Kantishna. Confronting Fannie and her obvious comfort with her life in the wilderness forced these men to find a way to accommodate her experience in their own narratives. Their approaches were to either masculinize Fannie or to put her experience into a domestic context.

In the meantime, by the 1920s, Fannie was well known among the women of Fairbanks. Even to these hardy women, she was exceptional in her abilities. "All through the years I had heard of this woman, . . . a real old timer, one of the early Klondike stampeders, who was better than most men at anything," said Lois McGarvey, who met Fannie in 1920. "I heard many tales of her hunting and bagging moose, dressing the huge animals, getting her team of dogs up and loaded for home. She brought in much fur every year and also had a mine for which she cut and hauled timbers with her dogs, fifteen to twenty miles up the steep mountainside."[7]

"It was not until 1920 that I again thought of my original plan with any degree of seriousness," wrote Lois in her book *Along Alaska's Trails*. "In late summer I had a call from one of my friends saying that a very well-known woman was coming in from the far distant place which was her home near Mt. McKinley; that she was to spend a few days in town, and my friend wanted to bring her down for tea." For some reason, Lois disguised the name of the well-known woman, calling her Hattie MacLain yet preserving her northern moniker as "Hattie the Hike."[8]

So Fannie came to tea. Lois made dainty tea sandwiches and delicate cupcakes. As she described the occasion:

> Hattie [Fannie] loved everything. She was a small built woman and middle aged. There was something about her that made one feel she resembled well-cured sinew. Her skin was brown and lined and the muscles of her arms showed though her sleeves. When she arrived with my friend, she was wearing an old fashioned brown dress and her snow pacs. As we were finishing out food, she picked up every crumb from her plate and ate it. She said, "I believe in folk' cleaning up their plates. Nothing makes me madder than to have people push this to the edge of their plates, and that to the edge of their plates and leave it!"[9]

Fannie invited Lois to visit her home, so Lois hired a dog team and driver to take her into Kantishna early in November. Lois's rich observations provide a detailed look at Fannie's daily life (of course, it was an edited version—she never mentioned Joe Quigley, for instance).

Lois and Fannie climbed Quigley Ridge, looking for fur signs in the fresh snow. From the top, Fannie pointed out her trapline, a long oval loop with both ends joining at the home cabin. The distance around the trapline was about 40 miles. After this one climb, Lois was so stiff and sore she begged for a day off, but Fannie's idea of recovery was to walk off the lameness, and she told Lois that she would get used to it if she stayed around for a while.

Fannie was well known to Mary Lee Davis, who had been a Fairbanks resident for only a few years when she traveled out to Kantishna in 1921.[10]

The Conquering of
by Belmore
of the Parker-

EDITOR'S NOTE.—*This is the story of a made against big odds. Mt. McKinley, North America and Mr. Browne and summit. Mt. McKinley is not the highest to climb. Every record peak rises paratively slight; but storm-swept Mt. from an Alaskan wilderness, almost incivilization whence every ounce of provision Browne expedition was full of stirring*

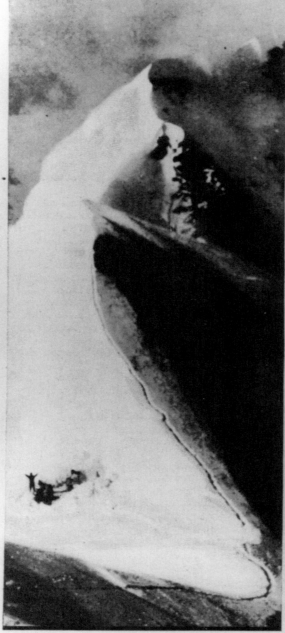

PHOTO BY BELMORE BROWNE

Looking up the northeast ridge, the only feasible approach to the summit. At times the party had to zigzag and chop steps in the ice

THERE is only one workmanlike way to reach the northern face of Mt. McKinley—in the winter time with dog sleds.

Professor Herschel C. Parker and the writer had exhausted every other promising approach. In 1906 we had studied the western and southwestern ridges, and in 1910 we had explored the excessively rugged glaciers and mountains of the southern approach. During the latter explorations we had tried the mountain at several different points between the southwestern, southern, and southeastern ridges, and on one of these attempts we reached our highest altitude of 10,300 feet. The problem of telling whether or not any particular route to the summit of this great peak is feasible, is far more simple than one would suppose. For Mt. McKinley rises to such a high altitude that unless the climbers find a route where they can camp and transport their food and shelter, their efforts would fail at the beginning.

Almost every high mountain in the world rises from a high base. In South America, for instance, the actual climbing of a 20,000 foot peak generally begins at an altitude of 16,000 feet, or over. Whereas Mt. McKinley rises from a base of from four to five thousand feet, leaving

Mt. McKinley

Browne
Browne Expedition

plucky fight such as any man likes, the fight
reaching 20,450 feet is the highest peak in
Prof. Parker got to within 200 feet of the
est mountain in the world but it is the hard-
from a high base; the actual climbing is com-
McKinley rises a bleak and sheer 15,000 feet
accessible, and hundreds of miles from any
must be hauled. The attempt of the Parker-
events well worth the telling and the reading

15,000 feet of snow and ice to be
negotiated. This fact makes Mt.
McKinley the highest peak in the
world above the line of perpetual
snow.

No possible route to the summit
existed on any of the slopes seen
by Professor Parker and the writer
in 1906 and 1910. We decided,
therefore, to make a third attack
from the northeastern side of the
big peak.

We were actuated by
two especial motives; the
ascent of Mt. McKinley, and the crossing
and exploration of the rugged and unknown portion of the Alaskan
Range lying just east
of Mt. McKinley.
To accomplish

"The Conquering of Mt. McKinley." The opening spread of Belmore Browne's account of the Parker-Browne expedition shows the very masculine portrayal of the East Coast–based explorers. *Outing Magazine. UAF Francis P. Farquahar collection*

The spunky East Coaster who fancied herself adventurous and the cantankerous wilderness woman spent eleven days together. From the account Mary Lee recorded in *We Are Alaskans,* it is apparent that Fannie talked her ear off. "And can she talk!" said Mary Lee. "Thank fortune all the farness and the stillness haven't quieted Fannie's good gift of fervent speech." But in the end, Mary Lee could not bring herself to actually write down what Fannie said. She described it instead as "dramatic, cogent, full of keen figurative language that is fairly Shakespearean in its rugged raciness."[11] Lois McGarvey termed Fannie's vocabulary "rich and forceful (but not printable)."[12]

As Davis related: "I listened while Fannie talked, and all the panorama of the West and North unrolled to Fannie's telling. She is herself a little less-than-five-foot library of all that's worth while in Alaska's past and future." Fannie must have started talking first thing in the morning, as she made sourdough griddle cakes, and continued on while they climbed the steep hills with pack dogs. When they returned to the cabin near dark, Mary Lee said, "Fannie unwearied and bustling about supper-getting, would laugh at me and my exhaustion."[13]

Fannie talked philosophy, told stories, shared nature lore and her knowledge of geology, and wore out her visitors as they hiked up and down the steep hills. Despite the stream-of-consciousness style of Davis's reportage, it is unlikely that the passages she put in quotes were truly remarks that she copied down at the time. Instead I think we have to view such remarks as partly reconstructed from memory and partly characterization by Mary Lee, such as this passage attributed to Fannie regarding the Dall sheep:

> "Eagles is about their only enemy, and eagles is bad, too, for foxes and spawning salmon. Eagles is death on the little long leggedy lambs, that are dropped along about in June. Wolves get them at the springs, sometimes, but the little lambs don't go down to water at first, ever. Their ma tucks 'em away under a rock and says—'now kids, you just stay put, and don't you budge or squeak mind, 'til I get back. You hear me?' And there they stay. I've come on 'em once or twice, and I can swear they sure do mind their ma's! They won't move a muscle, even when you're right on top of 'em. Then, like as not, on your way down you'll see a comical old ewe peeking at you round a rock—wondering did you harm her baby!"[14]

Davis portrayed Fannie as the archetypal Alaskan, resourceful, tough as nails, making a civilized paradise in the wilderness. Her gender was seemingly insignificant, or perhaps the fact that even women were tough was a badge of honor to Alaskans.

Lois McGarvey, who failed in her attempt as a beginning trapper, was another woman who both believed in and exemplified this same vision of Alaska as a place for anyone to test their limits, not just men.

Nannie Biddle, the wife of a Philadelphia lawyer, was one of many women searching for meaning in her life, as a woman, and looking for another example. In 1929, she began planning an expedition to "to study the customs and living conditions of Alaskan women."[15] To bolster her claim of being a serious researcher, rather than simply a runaway wife, she consulted Vilhjalmur Stefansson, Harold McCracken, and Dr. Grafton Burke, of Fort Yukon. She took with her movie and still cameras, two guns, and a sleeping bag, planning to write articles and perhaps a book. She left New York in December 1931, traveled by train to Seattle, took a boat to Seward, and then caught a train to Nenana, arriving in time to be the guest of honor at a New Year's dance.

Biddle was a prominent enough socialite to merit the attention of the *New York Times* as her journey progressed. In Nenana, she hired Mike Cooney to take her to Kantishna with his team of nineteen sled dogs but then had to wait two weeks while the temperatures hovered near 30° below zero. When the weather warmed a bit, they took off, and the news of her departure on January 16 was cabled to the *Times*. Although she undoubtedly never planned to stay more than a few weeks with Fannie, winter weather conspired to extend her stay. Mike Cooney made numerous attempts to reach Kantishna, but snow drifts and renewed storms prevented him from succeeding. The story was big enough that the *Pittsburgh Press* reported Nannie Biddle was still with Fannie on March 22, after talking to Joe Quigley's brother in nearby Kittanning, Pennsylvania. "A bitter Alaskan winter continued today to hold Mrs. Edward Biddle a prisoner in the tiny cabin of Joseph Quigley and his wife," the paper reported, continuing, "Since Mrs. Biddle was snowed in with the Quigleys three months ago, Cooney and his malamutes have been turned back time and again by vicious storms." After relating various details of the Quigleys' life, the article finished by reassuring readers that "she is suffering no hardship as long as she is with Joe and Fannie Quigley." Actually, whether Joe was there is uncertain: he had been in Fairbanks at the Alaska Hotel on January 15, as Nannie Biddle left for Kantishna.[16]

Nannie Biddle finally arrived in Fairbanks by plane on April 5, and the *News-Miner* was able to obtain an interview with her. Headlined "Alaska Enthralls Mrs. Biddle," the article described the trip as "a lifelong ambition satisfied." The interview was surprisingly short on real details about the three-month stay with Fannie, saying only, "Mrs. Biddle had many words

Plane to Try Society Woman's Rescue If Dogs Fail

Left, Mrs. Edward Biddle; top center, Mr. and Mrs. Joseph Quigley at their cabin; lower center, Quigley and his dog team; right, Mrs. Quigley.

Kittanning Native Helps Mrs. Biddle

Brother of Gold Miner, Resident of Verona, Tells of Primitive Led by Couple Who Are Entertaining Snowbound Society Woman

A bitter Alaskan winter continued today to hold Mrs. Edward Biddle a prisoner in the tiny cabin of Joseph Quigley and his wife, former Western Pennsylvanians, at the foot of Mt. McKinley.

Mike Cooney's eight-dog team is battling through the drifts in an attempt to reach the isolated Quigley home at Kantishna.

BANDITS KIDNAP SECOND VICTIM

2 Take $12 From Gas Station Attendant; Staged Other Holdup, Police Think

Kidnaped by two men, a Swissvale service station attendant was ... and ejected from the ...

The saga of the adventurous Philadelphia socialite Mrs. Nannie Biddle was featured in this clipping from a Pennsylvania newspaper in 1931. *UAF Fannie Quigley Collection*

of praise for Fannie Quigley . . . 'She is great[;] we got along beautifully[.] She has kept her sense of balance wonderfully out there on the real frontier.'" Biddle described the winter as unique and thrilling, mentioned taking many pictures of moose and caribou, and remarked on the gorgeous scenery viewed from the Quigley cabin. And that is it! It is so frustrating and yet so intriguing to try to picture what on earth Fannie found to do for three months with the forced companionship of a disenchanted society woman from Philadelphia. Perhaps not surprisingly, Nannie Biddle separated from and then divorced her husband not much more than a year after her return from the North. As far as I have been able to tell, she never wrote the book she had planned.[17]

CREATING THE PARK

Back in January 1908, during his winter on the Toklat River, Charles Sheldon had envisioned the high passes north of Mount McKinley as a wildlife reserve and national park. After returning from his Alaskan adventures, he married and settled in Washington, D.C., where he worked full-time with the Game Preservation Committee of the Boone and Crockett Club, representing the interests of its elite members on matters of public policy. The bill to establish the park, introduced in 1916, was passed in 1917, following the creation of the National Park Service itself, which was accomplished in August 1916. Sheldon informally proposed the idea of the Mount McKinley National Park to the new Park Service director, Stephen Mather, in a letter on Boone and Crockett Club Game Preservation Committee letterhead. Then supporters shrewdly allowed Judge Wickersham, by now elected as Alaska's nonvoting delegate to the House of Representatives, to introduce the bill. Tensions between the territorial residents and what they

Naturalist and big game hunter Charles Sheldon, during the winter he spent in the area that is now Denali National Park. *UAF William Sheldon Collection 76-42-4*

considered the eastern establishment were already a factor. Mindful of Alaskans' desire for home rule, Washington supporters knew that mining territory would have to be excluded from the area to be designated as a park. The club members had already run into resistance in 1908 while working on the federal level to strengthen Alaska's game codes. Thus, the bill to establish the park also included an unusual provision allowing the miners of the Kantishna to hunt game in the park on a subsistence basis. A park proposal that had not included provisions for local subsistence hunting would have encountered a "political minefield of strenuous opposition in Alaska."[18]

Harry Karstens, with some of the McKinley Park dogs in 1926. Karstens, the first superintendent of Mount McKinley National Park, inaugurated the use of dog teams by the park service. *NPS-DENA*

To further the cause and explain the motivations of park advocates, Belmore Browne, working under the auspices of the Camp Fire Club, authored a booklet that outlined the basic rationale for the new national park, closely following the pattern of the wilderness and game preservation dialogue of the day.[19] Whereas the booklet idealized the mountain wilderness and game preserve, the committee hearing concentrated on hunting, as congressional committee members objected to the hunting provisions. Park

supporters wanted to preserve wildlife and wildlife habitat, but they knew that in order to persuade the members of Congress, they would also have to present the whole idea as one of economic development and tourism.[20] The bill to create the park passed Congress and was signed by the president in February 1917. But the signing of the bill actually did not change anything in Kantishna. Not until 1921 was Harry Karstens appointed as the first superintendent. Then, gradually, the first park rangers and a few tourists began to venture into the park.

As mentioned earlier, Grant Pearson first met Fannie in 1926 when he was a young ranger and a relative newcomer in the ways of wilderness living. Hired by Harry Karstens, he was subjected to Harry's true test for fitness as a McKinley park ranger—a solo trip in the winter. Having survived that trial, Pearson was sent on a winter patrol through the park by dog

Grant Pearson, who started his career as a park ranger under Harry Karstens, rose to become superintendent of Mount McKinley National Park. *NPS-DENA*

team, and that is where he first met Fannie, who, of course, had already been perfecting her wilderness skills for some twenty years. "She always had a bed of grass for a visitor's dogs," Pearson wrote later. "She gathered grass in the summer, dried it, and kept it handy." But she told him, "By god, it is for the dogs I do this, not for you bums of rangers!"[21]

The construction of the Park Road was one of the most interesting and important efforts in the park, one that would change the park forever and shape its future. From the beginning, Belmore Browne, Charles Sheldon, James Wickersham, and other park supporters advocated the creation of the park as a tourist destination. All the witnesses in the congressional hearings mentioned this, as well. As a tourist destination, the park would bring business to the railroad, which from its inception had promoted its tours to Mount McKinley, and it was realized early on that providing access to the interior of the park would be key in attracting tourists. The thinking at the time was that if tourists could not access the park, then Congress would be reluctant to provide future funding. And of course, the few tourists who ventured on the tours wanted to see Mount McKinley, which is not visible from McKinley Park Station, the entrance to the park from the railroad. "Not only are there absolutely no accommodations within the park, but there are no roads, and at present, not even a well constructed trail," wrote park supporters in attempting to secure funding for the road.[22]

At the same time, development boosters throughout Alaska pushed for improved transportation and access. The Alaska Road Commission in the Department of the Army, originally under the direction of the flamboyant Gen. Wilds P. Richardson, supervised construction and maintenance on territorial roads. The miners in Kantishna and their supporters in Nenana continued to lobby for improved access. By 1921, the ARC, under Col. James G. Steese, suggested to Stephen Mather, Park Service director, that the ARC and the Park Service should cooperate in the building of a road through the park to meet the needs of both miners and tourists.

The Park Service saw the road primarily as a scenic route. The miners, however, had misgivings about the concept of joint use from the beginning, and they urged the upgrading of their winter trail to the railhead, known as the Lignite-Kantishna route.[23] But the Park Service was in Washington, whereas the miners were far away. And in the National Park Service, Colonel Steese saw a dedicated source of funding that would not compete for scarce resources with the other much-needed roads throughout Alaska. Efforts soon focused on a trail through the park over the four high passes that formed a natural route to the western boundary. In the sometimes rocky collaborative arrangement to build the road, which wound up

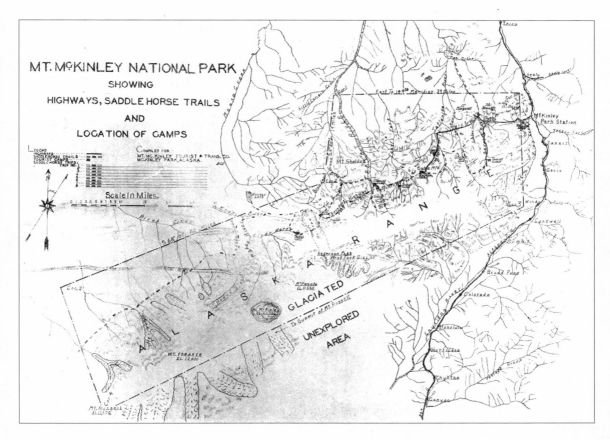

Map of Mount McKinley National Park, 1929. From *Farthest North Collegian* 7, no. 3, June 29, 1929, 8. *UAF*

taking sixteen years, the ARC, with its experience in building for Alaskan conditions, acted as contractor for the Park Service, often working under the direction of Park Service engineers and landscape architects more interested in scenic views than mining access.

In 1922, the ARC officially began the road project by marking and brushing the trail from McKinley Park Station to Wonder Lake. Tripods and mileage signs marked the route, and tents with stoves were erected for shelter at 12- to 15-mile intervals. Steese's hope for dedicated funding turned out to be a mirage, always apparently out there in the distance but only rarely appearing in reality. From the point of view of the ARC, it was Congress and the Park Service that kept the project from meeting its original schedule. The road was constructed in fits and starts, with crews pushing out into the park mile by mile and then going back in subsequent years to improve what had already been roughed out. By 1927, the road had pushed through the 34 miles to Igloo Creek. By 1929, it was suitable for traffic to East Fork.

Mrs. A. W. Lilliedale took advantage of the new road to visit her Kantishna claims in the summer of 1930, carrying a pack weighing 28 pounds, according to the *Daily News-Miner:* "She rode on an A.R.C. truck to the

East Fork of the Toklat and from there she packed across streams and mountains. The water was very high and it rained most of the time." Mrs. Lilliedale herself told the paper: "The road work is progressing rapidly and the road is a great help to the Kantishna." Apparently, she was welcomed to eat at the construction camps, as she also reported that "the camps have fine cooks and sure put up good feeds."[24]

After 1929, the project seemed to progress more smoothly, and it was completed in stages across the East Fork, over the "highline" blasted out of the rock through Polychrome Pass, and down to the Toklat River. The trestle bridge over the Toklat River, which, at half a mile, was the longest bridge on the road, was completed in 1931 as the road pressed ahead over Highway Pass. After visiting Wonder Lake, which was then outside the park boundary but had been proposed for inclusion, National Park Service director Horace Albright came to favor the construction of a hotel there, an idea that necessitated further changes in the road alignment.[25] The Wonder Lake area was added to the park in a 1932 expansion, and the road plan was extended to the new northwest boundary. The total of 88 miles of road was substantially complete to the northwest boundary, 5.5 miles south of Kantishna, by the end of the 1937 season and extended to Kantishna and the airstrip the following year.

The road project brought more visitors and new friends to Kantishna. Morgan Edmonds became the ARC superintendent for the project in the

Fannie with visitors, including Mr. and Mrs. Edmonds on horseback. Edmonds was working on the Park Road for the Alaska Road Commission. *UAF Fannie Quigley Photo Collection 80-46-225*

1930s. He was an Alaskan old-timer who had arrived in Fairbanks in 1908 as a prospector and miner after working as a surveyor for the Canadian Pacific. Edmonds worked on the construction of the Alaska Railroad between 1918 and 1921 and then moved to the ARC in 1922. He and his wife paid frequent visits to Fannie during those years and were often pictured with her, sometimes on horseback, having ridden the horses from the Savage River Tourist Camp.

Mr. Edmonds, Fannie, Mrs. Edmonds, geologist Philip Smith, and Joe Quigley. *UAF Fannie Quigley Photo Collection 80-46-242*

Selling Out

AFTER YEARS OF PRIVATION AND HARD WORK, **selling out was the Quigleys'** only goal. Yet Fannie realized that no matter how little money they had, at least they had enough to eat there in Kantishna, as she told her niece in a 1929 letter:

> Dear Teresa and Lewis,
>
> Will drop you few lines as I have not heared from you for long time. Airplane drop ar first class mail to day but there was no letter from non of you folks. I wrote to your mother last Sept. but it is here yet, plane did not land. They will be someone going out now soon as the rivers are closing up now. We will not go to town this winter it coust to much. We would like to go out siad but we can not go until we sale this place out got to have money to live out there and here we have best of meat and vegetables but we have got little money Will teresa there is no news here but worke hoping this will fine you both well and the children
>
> Your ant and uncle
>
> Fannie, Joe
>
> Will address this to your mothers place.[1]

But the letter also conveyed a sense of wistfulness, a loneliness exasperated by poor communication and transportation—the letters written but not mailed unless someone went out to town, the lack of money to go "outside" themselves or even to town. Fannie's abilities had given the Quigleys a good life, with "the best of meat and vegetables," which was no minor accomplishment. But it came at a cost, "no news here but worke." Joe and Fannie were truly partners in the enterprise of developing the mines, and now they were hoping to sell out.

The Quigleys had developed a routine by the early summer of 1930: Fannie tended the garden at their main cabin overlooking Friday Creek and continued her rounds of subsistence activities while Joe continued prospecting and developing new claims on the other side of the ridge, hoping to develop another paying mine. One day at the end of May 1930, Fannie made her customary 4-mile hike with fresh bread from the cabin over to the tunnel Joe was working on at his Banjo claim. But this was to be a day like no other. When she arrived, she found Joe in the small shack at the mine portal, seriously injured. Caught in a cave-in deep in the tunnel, he had somehow dragged himself back to the shack. Perhaps the inevitable had finally caught up to him after years of tunneling into these steep hillsides. Miles from help, there was little Fannie could do immediately besides making Joe as comfortable as possible. Then she hurried back over the 4-mile trail to Kantishna to summon help from the neighboring miners.[2]

Five or six of the miners followed her back up the hill to where Joe lay injured. Meanwhile, miner Billy Taylor hiked the 40 miles to the end of the construction on the Park Road, reaching the closest phone that could summon an airplane. The phone rang at midnight in Fairbanks, and pilot Joe Crosson took off an hour and a half later in a New Standard open-cockpit plane with Dr. Rex Swartz. Taylor had advised him to be prepared to amputate. Luckily, the plane made a successful landing on the Moose Creek Bar, where they met the patient. Joe's friends had improvised a splint for his leg and then carried the 6-foot, 4-inch miner on an improvised stretcher over the 4 miles to the airstrip. In order to stuff Joe's lanky frame into the open cockpit, Dr. Swartz had to remove the splint, causing Joe considerable pain. Joe finally arrived at the hospital in Fairbanks on June 2, where he was found to have broken his upper left femur near the hip and badly injured his shoulder. A long article in the Fairbanks paper announced that he would remain in the hospital there until the middle of September. Meanwhile, back at the mine, Fannie faced a summer with all of the usual preparations for winter subsistence, but now, for the first time, she would have to do it all without Joe.

"I don't know what I would have done if it hadn't been for the dogs," she wrote in a letter to Mary Lee Davis. "We got four now." And then she

Friends arrive with a stretcher to carry Joe Quigley back to the Kantishna airstrip after he was injured in a mine cave-in. *NPS-DENA*

detailed the myriad activities that had become her usual routine: "I have good garden—lettuce heads like cabbage—nice strawberries and so many all kinds berries. And I got big moose, dresses about eight hundred pounds. It was very fat. And some good fat caribou—one white like sheep. They will have road to Copper Mountain next fall. They have telephone there now. Went down six miles to-day for some meat I killed. Then I have about fifteen cords wood to haul, so you see when night comes I am tired."[3] After the experience of trying to get Joe out after his accident with no phone to summon help, access to a road and a phone took on new importance. But as in the years before, her routine was one of endless work—hauling the meat she killed 6 miles from home, hauling the 15 cords of wood.

Fannie and Joe's Friday Creek cabin in the winter, ca. 1930. Photo by Joe Quigley. *UAF Fannie Quigley Photo Collection 80-46-264*

Joe was ready to return home on September 10. But even with the new airplanes, transportation in that part of the world was difficult. On his first trip out with Alaskan Airways pilot Ed Young, they got close enough to buzz the cabin but could not land because the Moose Creek airstrip was under water.[4] So Joe remained in Fairbanks until September 24, and Fannie had two more weeks of hauling meat and wood and preparing for winter on her own. And then, even when Joe returned, he was unable to accomplish many of the routine tasks. Now Fannie had a partner who was partially disabled and needed her care.

Fannie *(center)*, with pilot Joe Crosson *(right)* and his wife, Lillian. *UAF Fannie Quigley Photo Collection 80-46-86*

Fannie wrote Mary Lee Davis in December 1930, continuing her litany of hard work. "They got his leg set three inches too long and he can't put his arm up to his head. I have to rub his arm and leg an hour every night and every morning and do all work now, for he can't even cut wood. So everything is up to me." But Joe was healing, as Fannie noted, "Joe is getting along very good. He walks about eight miles every day." And Joe added, "I must try to get to work soon, or I might get to like this invalid business."[5]

In March, pilots Percy Hubbard and Emil Jacobs demonstrated just how much closer Kantishna was to the rest of the world now when they flew from Fairbanks and dropped in on Fannie and Joe for lunch. Uncertain about the Moose Creek gravel bar, they had landed at Wonder Lake and hiked the 4 miles to the Quigleys' cabin. "Had fine visit with Mr. and Mrs. Quigley," they reported to the newspaper. "Mrs. Quigley is in best of health, but Mr. Quigley is not fully recovered from injuries he received last year. His leg and arm still bothering him, and he has not been able to do any development work at the mine, but expects to start work soon. . . . Little activity in Kantishna, at present," they noted, "and the trappers have light catches." Hubbard and Jacobs took off in late afternoon and were back in Fairbanks by 7:30 p.m.[6]

FROM CLAIM TO MINE

Following the abortive attempts to sell out in the early 1920s, Joe continued his efforts to attract potential investors. One person he managed to interest was Gen. A. D. McRae of Vancouver, one of the richest men in western Canada.[7] As the Depression deepened after 1929, McRae evaluated all possible investments and decided that gold mines in Alaska had the potential to be the most profitable. To assist him in evaluating prospects, he engaged longtime mining engineer and mining consultant Ira Joralemon.[8]

Although McRae and the Quigleys could both be said to be in the mining business, there could not be more of a contrast in their relative positions. The Quigleys had invested their entire lives in the Kantishna District and especially the prospects on Quigley Ridge. In effect, they had made an all-or-nothing bet. Thus, it was understandable that for them and others in a similar position, the arrival of a major capitalist god such as McRae frequently inspired false hopes; miners—and the town boosters who also stood to profit—often believed that the investor's option was a sure sign of his faith in the claim.

Wealthy investors such as McRae, by contrast, were constantly on the lookout for prime investments. They evaluated many mines and properties dispassionately based on their potential for profitable development, and they might buy options on multiple properties at one time. With the rights secured by the options and with access to capital, they could afford to sink more shafts, get accurate assays, and mill test loads of ore. They could do all this even in the face of a possible loss, hedging their bets by scattering chips across the board, knowing that another prospect would come along. Toward the end of his long career, Joralemon estimated that he had looked at thousands of properties and that only one out of every thousand prospects would become a paying mine.[9]

On McRae and Joralemon's first visit to the Quigleys' properties in September 1931, Fannie showed them around the prospects. But as Joralemon later explained, "I found the property interesting, but most important tunnels were filled to the roof with green ice so I couldn't really tell much. Nothing could be done anyhow until Joe came back so we had to tell Fannie that we couldn't take an option or make a payment that year."[10] (Although Joe had been in Kantishna for much of the spring of 1931, he may have gone outside Alaska for medical treatment at this time.) Nonetheless, Joralemon suspected that McRae gave Fannie an informal payment for an option, without any contract, as he often did. Joralemon remarked that he had heard McRae say on several previous occasions that a miner "needs it more than I do, so I'll give him the payment anyhow," and he speculated that a little extra cash would have helped Fannie survive comfortably.[11]

McRae and Joralemon got back to Kantishna two years later along with local mining expert Ernest Patty, whom McRae had hired as Alaska manager. It was the beginning of a long association for the two mining men. Patty, a respected professor of mining engineering at the University of Alaska School of Mines (and later president of the university) was familiar with the Quigley claims and the Kantishna conditions, and he smoothed the way for McRae and his enterprises. Joe Quigley met them in Fairbanks, and the group flew to Wonder Lake. This time, McRae was ready to offer money. Joe and Fannie both signed the option with him, and he gave them each a check for half of the $15,000 cash payment. McRae contracted for development work almost immediately, engaging Joseph Snyder and Henry Mudge to drill a 1,000-foot tunnel into the Red Top vein.[12]

Joralemon and McRae returned to Kantishna again in July 1934, after Patty had arranged to have the ice chipped out of the Little Annie tunnel. But testing had shown that the Little Annie ore samples were hopelessly low-grade and, in addition, that a thrust fault cut off the principal vein. There was not enough ore to be worth the cost of development in such a remote location. McRae gave up his option.[13]

In spite of what would seem to be bad news, Joe said he was "feeling quite optimistic" as he passed through Fairbanks on his way outside in December 1934. Specifically, he mentioned that "during the past season I have been doing development work and bringing my property along until at present I have a pretty fair idea of what I have there." Undoubtedly, he had already begun discussions with the next group of investors, but he kept the details under his hat. Speaking in general, Joe added, "There are a number of promising looking showings in the district that need a bit more development before the owners are warranted in putting on milling equipment, but that will come in time." He also said that a considerable amount of development work would be done over the winter. "I am still having a bit of trouble with my arm," he told the Fairbanks paper, "and may take a trip to Seattle to have the doctor look it over again. Mrs. Quigley will stay at the property during my absence and look after our affairs."[14]

District Mining Commissioner Charles Trundy, passing through Fairbanks in March 1934, echoed Quigley's optimism. He said he anticipated a bright future for the district, citing the price of gold and the extension of the Park Road, which was still under construction: "The road will be built through to Wonder Lake this year, and next year right into Kantishna Mining District. Then watch that camp grow."[15] In fact, this time, faith in the district was not misplaced. As the larger investors pulled out, changing economic parameters were beginning to make the properties more attractive for local investors.[16]

In 1935, Quigley leased his Banjo Lode gold claim to local investors Ernest R. Fransen and Clifton M. Hawkins, both longtime hard rock men in the Fairbanks District. Although outside investors had not taken up the Quigleys' claims and the railroad had not changed the economics of the galena ore there, the interior was enjoying a mining resurgence, generating cash in the local economy. The newspaper was fairly clear as to the cause, as indicated in the headline: "Higher Price of Gold Aids Mining Work." In truth, the mining resurgence had begun with the railroad, bringing in major investments in large-scale mechanized placer mining with funding by the Boston-based U.S. Smelting, Refining, and Mining Company (USSR&M). Through the subsidiary Fairbanks Exploration Company, USSR&M bought thousands of acres of placer claims and built ten huge gold dredges. "Not since the boom days of the early Nome and Fairbanks and other camps has interior Alaska enjoyed such activity in its placer fields as this year."[17] Fairbanks was in the midst of a new boom, even as the rest of the country was racked by the Depression. In the midst of the Depression, President Franklin Roosevelt declared the dollar convertible to gold at a new price of $35 an ounce, increasing the value of gold from $20.67 an ounce (or devaluing the dollar, depending on one's point of view).

Along with the placer boom came a renewed interest in the hard rock, or "quartz," claims, as they were known locally. "Increased Price for Gold and Machinery Efficiency Encourage Hard Rock Work: Gold Veins Being Developed throughout the Interior" reported the paper.[18] Among the most successful of the hard rock mines was the Hi-Yu, the property that Fransen managed. So the purchasers of the Quigley mines knew what they were doing, and Fransen already had a good reputation in Fairbanks as a manager.

Local investors now had money and experience, which, together with the rising price of gold, substantially changed the economic incentives. Fransen and Hawkins later purchased seventeen patented claims from Fannie and Joe, and with Fairbanks businessman A. Hjalmer Nordale, they formed the Red Top Mining Company.[19] So, ironically, it was not the galena claims that Joe had worked on for years but the gold claims—the last claims Quigley developed, high on the south side of the ridge dividing Friday and Eureka creeks—that became a significant mine. This turn of events underscored the importance of timing and external events in the development of a successful mine operation.

The development of the Red Top Mine between 1935 and 1939 was part of a new mining boom in Alaska, as the *Fairbanks Daily News-Miner* noted in the November 1939 special "Goldfields Edition." The paper was fairly clear that the increased value of gold was the genesis of the boom, explaining, "Under the incentive of the higher price of gold hundreds of miles of placer gold properties in Alaska hitherto of too low grade to be worked are now made profitable, and scores of quartz properties are likewise affected."[20] Actually, the coming of the railroad with cheaper fuel and improved technologies had an equal effect. Yields for gold were at record levels, thanks to the use of the new technologies: "In a record smashing mechanized mining drive, Alaska is going over the top this year with a magnificent gold yield and a splendid production in other minerals." The new investment in equipment, including draglines, quartz drills, tractors and bulldozers, and milling machinery, particularly benefited Fairbanks businesspeople: "The season of 1937 has witnessed the greatest importation of mechanized mining equipment into Fairbanks and other Interior Alaska camps known in history. It is estimated that five million dollars worth of mining equipment has come into Alaska most of it into interior Alaska this season. Authoritative sources indicate 15,000 tons of equipment will come into Fairbanks this winter, and that 1938 will witness a banner year in mining exploration development importation of supplies and general traffic and activities."[21]

It was in this context that the *News-Miner* ran the story "Quigley Quartz Property in Kantishna Being Developed on a Large Scale," noting that "more than three miles of quartz claims, most of them patented, changed ownership in the transaction." The paper further credited Quigley with having driven "more than 3,000 feet of tunnel" in the course of development work, started in 1912.[22] By the fall of 1938, the company had built 5 miles of road, assay shop, bunkhouses, and a blacksmith shop, and it was getting ready for delivery of a 50-ton ball mill. After a satisfactory test of the mill in late 1938, the company began full-scale production in 1939. The Red Top Mining Company thus controlled the majority of the Quigley ground, but in August 1937, Joe and Fannie optioned additional claims to W. E. Dunkle for $150,000.

The Red Top Mine prospered from 1939 until 1942. Especially in hindsight, the 1930s and 1940s were the golden era for mining in Alaska. And then, just as the mines and the park together seemed poised for prosperity, Roosevelt issued Executive Order E–208 shutting down all gold mining as nonessential to the war effort.

ELEVEN

Drifting Apart

FANNIE AND JOE'S RELATIONSHIP seems always to have confused both their visitors and those writing about them. To mining consultant Joralemon, Fannie was a paradox. On the one hand, he saw her as "a sweet, kindly looking old lady, like a New England grandmother." On the other hand, he noted that "though she was almost 60 years old in 1931 she took me around the steep trails at such a pace that I had to stop to look at rocks every few minutes to catch my breath."[1] Fannie's language had always been raw and raunchy, as indicated first by Mary Lee Davis, who described "Fannie's good gift of fervid vivid speech."[2] Lois McGarvey, the prospective trapper, could not even bring herself to repeat what Fannie had said while cussing her out after releasing a lynx.[3] Joralemon had his own description: "Her language was absolutely sulfurous! . . . An education even after hearing the Cornish miners in Arizona. Every now and then she would realize what she was saying and would turn around to say, 'Oh, excuse me! I just get that way from talking to the dogs.'"[4]

According to Joralemon, when he and General McRae returned to Kantishna in 1933, two years after Joralemon's prior visit, Fannie had aged markedly and mellowed as well, having lost her shrill edginess. "We found Fanny was much older looking and milder than she had been two years earlier, but she was still full of energy," he wrote in his memoir. But he also noted that she and Joe, though outwardly friendly to each other, fought too much to live together. As noted earlier, they both signed the option with McRae, and he gave them each a check for half of the $15,000 cash payment.[5] Years earlier, visitors to the couple's cabin had assumed they were married when they were not; now, Joralemon assumed they had never married, writing that "there were a few uncertainties of the legal status of a common-law wife," as they split McRae's option payment.[6]

In July 1934, Joralemon visited again and found Fannie and Joe looking much older and, to his eyes, failing rapidly. He said that Joe had spent the winter on a drive up the California and Oregon coasts, enjoying his $7,500. He also wrote that Fannie had gone to San Jose, California to spend the winter with a sister; however, he reported, "her language horrified them so much that she soon returned to Kantishna." Here, Joralemon was probably repeating a story he heard from one of his contacts, as there is really no evidence that Fannie ever left Alaska after 1924. The *News-Miner* reported that Joe and Fannie arrived in Fairbanks from Kantishna in July 1934 and stayed at the Alaska Hotel as "Mr. and Mrs. Quigley." In spite of the fact that McRae gave up his option, Joe was "feeling quite optimistic" as he passed through Fairbanks on his way outside in December that year, though he was still bothered by his previous injuries. Joe commented that again, Fannie would stay at their property during his absence.[7]

Indeed, in the years following Joe's 1930 accident, the Quigleys often lived apart, as Joe spent less and less time as a resident of Kantishna. It is likely that this is when Fannie's alcoholism began to be more noticeable. When Joe arrived in Fairbanks in the summer of 1935, he led a newspaper reporter to understand that he planned on visiting the larger town frequently, which perhaps was a subtle way of indicating his intention not to live in Kantishna at all.[8]

Just after New Year's Day in 1936, Fannie had her own accident. She was returning to Kantishna by train after a trip to Fairbanks and was invited to spend the night at the home of Park Superintendent Harry J. Liek and his wife. During the night, she fell down the basement stairs; she was flown back to the hospital in Fairbanks with a broken leg. By the next day, it was determined that a severe fracture just above the knee would require a three-month stay in the hospital.[9] In the years she had lived in the North, Fannie had never been confined to a room, let alone a bed. One can only imagine what she went through as she contemplated this confinement. To pass the time, she had her friends stop in with alcohol, and toward the end of her hospital stay, when the alcohol got to her or possibly when it ran out, she would scream and carry on in her famous outdoor voice, hoping to have her leg released from the traction apparatus, all to the consternation of one young Fairbanks girl who spent some of those months as Fannie's roommate.[10]

Meanwhile, in the sale of their claims to the Red Top Mining Company, Joe and Fannie received $100,000 plus 10 percent of gross. In April

1937, they agreed to split the proceeds deposited at First National Bank, and they finalized their separation with a divorce.[11]

Writing in 1947 in the *Alaska Sportsman Magazine*, Grant Pearson described the few weeks before Fannie died and stated that "Joe had been dead about seven years then."[12] Perhaps he thought he was adding to the sentimentality of the story, or perhaps a mistake was made by his editors. In any case, three years later, in a March 1950 article about Joe, Pearson referred to Fannie as his "first wife" and noted that he himself had seen Joe in Seattle in 1945! Actually, after the divorce, Joe had moved to Seattle and married Julia, a nurse he had met while rehabilitating from his injuries; he died in 1958.[13] But other writers, apparently using Pearson's earlier piece as a source, perpetuated his original mistake. I call attention to this misinformation because this and other stories have caused a great deal of confusion among historians trying to uncover the real facts of Joe's and Fannie's lives. It also amply illustrates the problems inherent in relying solely on secondary written accounts.

But oral histories have their own biases. Most of the stories told about Fannie in the mid-1930s and the recorded oral histories relating those stories tend to focus on her alcoholism. It seems that this was what people who knew Fannie in that period remembered about her. Yet the focus on her alcoholism threatens to overwhelm the other parts of her story.

As the Red Top Mining Company constructed its camp and facilities, George Bachner, the contractor, also built a small frame house close to the Moose Creek airstrip, where Fannie moved sometime after 1939.[14] During the few short years that the mine was under construction and in operation (from 1938 to 1942), Fannie was able to take advantage of the company's many flights to and from Fairbanks to visit town more frequently, and she probably did not have to depend on her own resources as she had before. In December 1937, for example, she and company employee Norman Crooks arrived in Fairbanks by plane.

From a thriving and prosperous mining camp, Kantishna was bounced back into a backwater in 1942 by Roosevelt's executive order shutting down mining. Fannie, seventy-two that spring, and her neighbor, the eccentric bachelor miner Johnny Busia, were left as the sole residents of the Kantishna Mining District. At the other end of the park, with civilian travel to Alaska curtailed by wartime restrictions, tourists disappeared, and park facilities were taken over by the armed forces for use as a rest-and-recreation camp for soldiers. This turn of events brought two final visitors to Fannie's home, the adventurer Virgil Burford and Maj. George Hall. Both had the military man's sense of wilderness as a testing ground for a new

Johnny Busia, Fannie's neighbor, with Joe Quigley in happier times. *NPS-DENA*

masculinity. And each devoted an entire chapter of his Alaska adventure book to Fannie. They each portrayed her as a peculiar, middle-gendered person, neither all male nor all female. Her risqué language and propensity for strong drink seemed to be her most remarked on features. Burford was the herald of the new generation of small-scale miners and 1960s back-to-the-land nature lovers who would flock to the wilderness in later years.[18]

Burford had decided to spend the summer mining for gold on Friday Creek, just below Fannie's cabin. "You dirty so-and-so! Get the hell out of here and stay out!" was her first greeting. Burford's description of Fannie herself and of her abode inscribed what would become the characteristic portrait of her:

> I stepped through the line of dogs, who set up a bedlam of barking at
> my approach, and into the open doorway. A woman sat at a sawed
> plank table drinking milky liquid from a tin cup. On the table before

her were a bucket of water and a jug. The jug's label read, "Grain Alcohol." She tipped up her head and said in a harsh, blunt voice, "Hello Jack! Pull up a chair and have a drink."

She was close to seventy that day I met her, a short, slight woman who weighed barely a hundred pounds. Her skin was wrinkled and weather-burned. The wisps of hair escaping from a man's battered felt hat were gray. She wore shoe pacs, khaki choke-bore pants and a checkered wool shirt.[19]

Again, in dress and behavior, Fannie was portrayed as both unisex and an anachronism. Yet there was much in the description that still embodied domesticity:

She brought out a loaf of homemade bread and a huge cold roast of caribou and a wedge of blueberry pie.

"Never saw a prospecting bum that wasn't starved," she snapped. "You eat that."

Within the range of her domestic activities, Fannie could include sharpening a pick:

She turned and shoved the blunt end into the open front of the stove and shook up the fire. When the metal finally turned red she carried the pick to the anvil and hammered the end expertly to a sharp point. "There—," she handed it back—"at least you got one thing right now."

Maj. George Hall, who spent some months in the park assigned to the military's recreation program, told a story about driving Fannie from the railroad station at McKinley Park Station to her cabin, 90 miles into the park, in the fall of 1943, just a year before her death. Unfortunately, by this time, everything he had come to admire about her was shaded by her drinking. The recollections of Fannie that he incorporated in his book were somewhat romanticized, but he at least seems to have recorded the cadence of her speech, laced with four-letter words—although even these quotes are probably a sanitized version.

Years in the far north had taught Fanny to check all items carefully before starting any trip. She remembered the day in 1908 when she hooked up the dog team, mushed thirty miles to her hunting cabin, only to discover that she had neglected to load the smoked salmon for the dog food.

"You fellers load a wagon like a bunch of che-chak-ers. Hell! If you loaded a bunch of dogs that way, they'd take one look at you and go shift for themselves."[20]

His account repeatedly mentioned Fannie's affinity for strong drink. Still, in a book otherwise filled with hunting, fishing, and bush pilots as representative of a masculine Alaska, Hall was obsessed with determining what was, indeed, womanly about this woman. So, though he repeated his version of her brash speech, "What the hell you gawking at?" he added, "Then she smiled that open friendly grin and becoming feminine for just a fleeting moment, said 'Hell I even bought a lady's hat when I was in town, a green one with a feather!'"[21]

As portrayed by Hall, with her gruff voice and blackened eye, Fannie was indeed a paradox. She refused to let him help her put on her sweater, saying, "I can still help myself." Despite what must have appeared to Hall as her age and infirmity, she was still the feisty woodswoman. However, by portraying himself as one who thought he had to be a gentleman around Fannie, Hall was exposing himself as unfamiliar with the customs of the country.

Finally arriving in the Kantishna country, just past the park boundary, Fannie insisted on opening a bottle of whiskey to greet Johnny Busia, the only other year-round resident. Noticing that the whiskey had a "great and friendly effect on her," Hall remarked, "I was beginning to think that she was a really a sweet old lady." Thus, in spite of her history in the mining camp, which he knew full well, he insisted on seeing this seventy-three-year-old woman in the mode of the familiar grandmotherly, sweet old lady. "If that damned Johnny Busia hasn't fed my dogs and cat I'll be damned if he is going to get a drink!" she said as they passed Wonder Lake and neared Kantishna, now a ghost town.[22]

"See those tire tracks in the road there, Kid? That means that Busia is out here some place getting wood. Don't drive so damn fast. We'll surprise him."

A few minutes more and Fanny's prediction became a fact. Just off the road stood a dilapidated Ford pick-up. Fanny cupped her wrinkled and gnarled hands to her lips, shouting, "Busia, Busia!" I stopped the truck as Johnny Busia carrying an axe over his shoulder, wearing a soiled blue shirt opened at the neck, strolled up to the truck from the opposite side of the road.

"What the hell you yelling at, old lady? Hello cap-I-tan."

"Why you damned old fool, I just stopped to buy you a drink. What in the hell have you done with my dogs? Poisoned them?"

The last thing she said to Hall, her "parting admonition," was: "Go-damit, kid, if you drive like you did coming out here, I'll probably never see you again!"[23]

Epilogue

F. Quigley Funeral Is End of Era

Chill gloomy rain beat against the small Tye-Phillips Funeral chapel
Thursday night as serious-faced crowds shuffled down the narrow
pathway to attend the last rites for Fannie Quigley, the droll, spunky,
tenacious little pioneer so well known and loved throughout Alaska.

Fannie died last week alone in her small rugged homestead at the
edge of McKinley Park.

An Immortal Legend

And thus she was given up to immortal legend, for so long as there is
an Alaska stories will be told and retold with gusto and admiration for
the lively mite of a woman whose famed personality, salty vigor and
great kindness are heart and sinew of the last frontier.[1]

As I was finishing the final draft of this volume, I returned to Fannie's
grave site in Birch Hill Cemetery, just north of Fairbanks. Twenty years
ago, on my first visit, the cemetery occupied a quiet hillside 2 or 3 miles out
of town with a view south to Mount McKinley, and it seemed a fitting place
for her burial. Now, the cemetery overlooks one of the busiest intersections
in Fairbanks. Just in the last three years, the once empty field has sprouted
a Home Depot, a Wal-Mart, and a Lowe's, and even more stores and restaurants are under construction. Ironically, these stores supply all of the goods

and conveniences that Fannie did without during her years in the Kantishna. In fact, in many ways, her life was defined by doing without. She made a life of what she did not have, and among her fellow pioneer women and others in Fairbanks, she was renowned for the life she made.

Fannie's obituary and the reports of her funeral had said that her legend would live on. And they were right, the legend did live on. But the woman behind the legend seemed to have disappeared. It was the inconsistencies in the stories that first attracted me to Fannie's history, all surrounding the major irony that so little was known about such a "legendary" character. I admit that at first, it was the tantalizing mistake regarding Fannie's marital state that intrigued me.

Ideas about marriage, gender roles, and sexuality were a particular casualty of the need to project the 1950s' gender roles back in time. When I arrived in Alaska in 1970, society was in the midst of cultural change, and the idea that men and women could live together as independent selves, cohabiting without the civil formality of marriage, was a new one.

Although many memoirs and first-person accounts had appeared in the thirty years or so after the gold rushes, Alaska's history began to be collected and compiled into a master narrative only in the 1950s. Writers of that era projected their particular values upon the earlier age, portraying the gold rush as a time and place of men and masculinity. Women were erased or set apart as singular and unusual, that is, not representative. The idea that the only women in the Yukon were prostitutes or that being a prostitute or a dance hall girl was the only available career option for women entered the popular consciousness. Indeed, this notion was so entrenched that the can-can girl is still the official emblem of the Klondike Visitor Association.[2] Pierre Berton's *Klondike Fever,* published in the 1960s, presented the era as a man's story. As an example, he focused on the story of Jack McQuesten and his fellow traders as the "Fathers of the Yukon," never investigating or mentioning the wives of the traders, the mothers of the Yukon. When women were not left out altogether, they were uniformly misrepresented as utterly dependent beings. In this context, Fannie was seen as a singular wilderness woman, while we are left to assume that all others were home taking care of the kids.

Without the facts, it was impossible to give Fannie and other women credit for their spirit of independence and adventure. It was impossible to understand Fannie's life or her role in the development of Alaska without understanding what other women were doing there. Thus, the first generations of writing on women in the North sought to recover the stories of women who had been left out of history. The notion was that if only we could recover the stories, then the significance would be understood, implicit in the resurrected tales. Through the research and writing of Melanie Mayer in *Klondike Women*, Francis Backhouse in *Women of the Goldrush*, Sally Zanjani in *A Mine of Her Own*, and my own work with Claire Murphy in *Gold Rush Women*, we now know that many women were, in fact, active participants and played a much larger role than previously thought.[3]

In the recovery phase of this enterprise, it was all about the facts, and the facts of women's lives were hard to come by. With many of these women sometimes having multiple husbands and numerous last names, it could be three times as much work to look through the common records. Furthermore, women often were not remembered in detailed obituaries in the way that men were, and they were frequently left out of common histories. When I began the work on Fannie, I thought that if only I could get the facts straight, then the story would be self-evident.

However, I have come to understand that the facts are only elusive guideposts. We may find information, dates, mining claims, records of trips to town, and more, but what does it all really mean? Historians are asking deeper questions about significance, meaning, and themes. The information to interpret the facts about Fannie can only come from the people who wrote about her and from an understanding of the personal motives that influenced how they chose to represent her.

Fannie was not an educated woman. Although I do have a few letters she wrote to her sisters after 1907, it seems that she was nearly illiterate when she arrived in the North. There is no diary, memoir, or first-person account at all. Thus, I have had to rely on the testimony of others who visited and then wrote about her, with all of their own agendas and prejudices. Many of those who wrote about Fannie were other women. What did she mean to them? Over the years, I have worked with reminiscences, memoirs, and "as told to" memoirs. So, in large part, Fannie's story is really the story of what she meant to other women: indeed, it can be read in terms of what women meant to each other. To women such as Lois McGarvey, Mary Lee Davis, Nannie Biddle, and Ruth Wilson Barrack, she seemed to have represented the limits of the possible.

There are tantalizing clues about the broad appeal Fannie's story had beyond Alaska. In June 1930, while Joe was recovering in the hospital in Fairbanks, the *Daily News-Miner* reprinted a letter he had written to the publisher of the *Lapeer County (Michigan) Press*.[4] The letter was a response to publicity Fannie had received in Michigan after the publisher visited them at the park.

> That story you wrote about Fannie and how she keeps house must have
> been interesting to many of the people out there for Fannie is still getting
> letters from women either asking her to let them know if there was such
> a woman existing that hunted, trapped and drove dogs like she did or else
> asking advice on how to come to Alaska and establish a home for them-
> selves. . . . After reading their letters I'm afraid that both Fannie and I
> would hesitate before visiting Lapeer for the people there might expect
> to see super human beings and we would hate to disappoint them.

Joe acknowledged here that the stories about Fannie portrayed her as a larger-than-life character, almost superhuman. In fact, she was so well known that, as Joe related, "one of the letters was just addressed to Fannie Quigley, interior of Alaska and yet she got it all right."

—⁓—

Many of the stories told about Fannie in the mid-1930s and the recorded oral histories relating those stories highlight her alcoholism. I have always believed that the emphasis on and repetition of these stories tends to misrep-resent Fannie's earlier years by portraying her as always a drunk. However, I have to acknowledge that it is equally possible that the stories present her accurately and that it is I who choose to romanticize Fannie's story by dis-counting them.

One part-time Kantishna resident remembered that Fannie used to order cases of booze to be delivered, probably on the planes flying in sup-plies for the Red Top Mining Company. When she got good and loaded she would sometimes go out and shoot off the tops of the neighborhood stovepipes. "We never worried for our safety," he said, "because she was a damned good shot."[5] Grant Pearson tells a story concerning Father Fitzger-ald, who, like many of the missionaries in the north, visited his far-flung parishioners by airplane. He and his pilot made an unplanned landing at Kantishna to avoid a gathering storm, and of course Fannie invited them to stay and served them her famous caribou stew. But Father Fitzgerald care-fully picked out the caribou and left it on the side of his plate

> "What in the hell's the matter," she exploded, "don't you like what I
> do to Caribou?"
> "You know today is Friday Mrs. Quigley. I don't eat meat."
> "I see," said Fannie and disappeared into the kitchen. She returned
> with a bowl of lettuce. "Here eat rabbit food. Rabbits are religious
> every day of the week."

Two views of the interior of the cabin near the Moose Creek airstrip where Fannie moved after 1939. *UAF Fannie Quigley Photo Collection 80-46-266 and 80-46-268*

The punch line came when the good-natured Father offered to pay for his stay, which of course Fannie refused.

> "Well, look here then, . . . after my pilot gets me to Fairbanks he'll be flying back past here. What kind of chocolates do you like?"
>
> "Schlitz." Fannie replied instantly.
>
> The next day the pilot came back with two cases of beer and a quart of whiskey.[6]

By the 1950s, Grant Pearson had become park superintendent and was settled into family housing, with a wife and child. In his heavily sentimentalized article about Fannie, his "most unforgettable character," Pearson could only project onto her the idea that she had missed much of what he felt life had to offer.

> She stood before the window at the Wonder Lake Ranger Station after having dinner with me and my family. Her great love for our little daughter was both beautiful and pathetic, and in her eyes we could see an intense longing for the sweet things of life she had missed.
>
> To some of those who visited her, Fannie was a sort of curiosity, which according to ordinary standards, she was indeed. But she was more than that to those who knew her. She was genuine, sincere, a truly great personality.[7]

Following Pearson's lead, accounts written after Fannie's death often sentimentalized her as a tough but ultimately pathetic woman. Genuine and sincere, certainly, but those very characteristics seemed only to provide dimension to her role as "colorful character" and in the end set her apart from those who truly lived in the modern world.

Johnny Busia found Fannie dead in her cabin on August 25, 1944. The newspaper never said whether her death was the result of her drinking, rendering her unable to light the fire she was building, or simply a heart attack. To most people in Fairbanks, it probably amounted to the same thing: natural causes. The obituary noted her ability to "work like a man and entertain like a queen," and her "industrious habits" and "success as a miner" still confounded easy classification, which no longer mattered in any case. It also stated that she had stayed in the Kantishna by choice, "where there was no need to lower her high ringing voice to conversational tones or to forsake her outdoor garb."

Fannie continued to garden even after her move to the cabin near the Moose Creek airstrip. Here she is shown in her large potato patch. *UAF Fannie Quigley Photo Collection 80-46-215*

In a long account of the funeral, which was conducted by the Pioneer Women of Alaska, the *News-Miner* piled on the adjectives, calling her a "droll, spunky, tenacious little pioneer, so well known and loved throughout Alaska."[8] "And thus she was given up to immortal legend," the readers were reminded, "for so long as there is an Alaska, stories will be told and retold with gusto and admiration for the lively mite of a woman whose famed personality, salty vigor and great kindness are heart and sinew of the last frontier."

NOTES

—⚬—

INTRODUCTION

1. Belmore Browne, "Hitting the Home Trail from Mt. McKinley," *Outing Magazine,* July 1913, 399.

2. *FDNM,* August 28, 1944.

3. Mary Lee Davis, *We Are Alaskans* (Boston: Wilde, 1931).

4. *FDNM,* August 28, 1944.

5. Extracted from records of Yukon Health and Human Resources; letter from Deputy Registrar of Vital Statistics, February 29, 1988.

OBITUARY

1. The obituary appeared in *FDNM,* August 28, 1944.

CHAPTER 1: NEBRASKA AND THE WEST

1. Dorothy Creighton, *Nebraska, a History* (Louisville: AASLH, 1977), 8.

2. Rose Rosicky, *History of Czechs in Nebraska* (Omaha: Czech Historical Society of Nebraska, 1929), 98, available online at http://www.rootsweb.com/~neethnic/czechs/contents.html (accessed September 24, 2006).

3. Census records. Although her obituary stated that "Fannie was born in Wahoo, Nebraska, March 18, 1871," there seems no doubt that Fannie had entered the world and was noticed and counted by the census taker in June 1870.

4. Rosicky, *History of Czechs in Nebraska,* 19.

5. Ibid.

6. Baptismal record, at Prague, NE, January 30, 1878.

7. Rosicky, *History of Czechs in Nebraska,* 160.

8. Bess Streeter Aldrich, *A Lantern in Her Hand* (1928; repr., New York: New American Library, 1989).

9. Ibid., 92–94.

10. Ibid., 99.

11. James C. Olson, *History of Nebraska* (Lincoln: University of Nebraska Press, 1966), quote from Addison Sheldon, 174.

12. Frank Cedja quoted in Rosicky, *History of Czechs in Nebraska*, 166, 162.

13. Rosicky, *History of Czechs in Nebraska*, 61–62.

14. Alan Bogue, *Money at Interest: The Farm Mortgage on the Middle Border* (Lincoln: University of Nebraska Press, 1969), 1–6.

15. Olson, *History of Nebraska*, 177.

16. The Bohemians in particular were generally well educated, fond of reading, and insistent on education for their children. The immigrant concept that the first generation of girls on the homesteads could not attend school because there was too much work to be done and because schools had not been established comes from Willa Cather, *My Ántonia* (New York: Houghton Mifflin, 1918).

17. Miscellaneous school documents, Saunders County Courthouse, Wahoo, NE.

18. Aldrich, *A Lantern in Her Hand*, 107.

19. Cedja quoted in Rosicky, *History of Czechs in Nebraska*, 161–64.

20. Nebraska State Census, 1885, NSHS.

21. Ibid.

22. Genealogical information, Family History Center, LDS Church. These records are well indexed and accessible through assistance at any Family History Center or online at www.familysearch.org (accessed September 24, 2006).

23. This was the real era and location of the sod house frontier, as pictured in the famous photographs of Solomon D. Butcher taken in Custer County between 1886 and 1891, now at the NSHS; and available online at www.loc.gov and www.nebraskahistory.org (accessed on September 24, 2006).

24. Bogue, *Money at Interest*, 72.

25. Vencil Sedlacek obituary, Burial 2 Apr 1921 Geranium Cem, Sargent, Valley, Nebraska. Obituary on microfilm at NSHS.

26. Ibid.

27. John Mack Farragher made this point in his social history, *Sugar Creek: Life on the Illinois Prairie* (New Haven, CT: Yale University Press, 1986).

28. Nebraska and Kansas had less than half the railroad mileage in 1913, but three years later, Kansas had 90 percent of the mileage it would have before World War I and Nebraska had more that 80 percent of its prewar mileage. See Richard White, *It's Your Misfortune but None of My Own* (Norman: University of Oklahoma Press, 1991), 250.

29. People of Saunders County, Nebraska, *Saunders County History* (Wahoo, NE: Saunders County Historical Society, 1983).

30. Maury Klein, *Birth of the Union Pacific* (Garden City, NY: Doubleday, 1987).

31. Josie and her new husband would later move west to Oregon; Mary got married and eventually moved to Anacortes, Washington.

CHAPTER 2: FANNIE THE HIKE

1. Claims are numbered and also designated as "Above" or "Below" the discovery claim.

2. Ethel Berry's story is documented in Claire Rudolf Murphy and Jane G. Haigh, *Gold Rush Women* (Seattle, WA: Alaska Northwest Books, 1997).

3. See especially Melanie Mayer, *Klondike Women: True Tales of the 1897–98 Gold Rush* (Athens, Ohio: Swallow Press/Ohio University Press, 1989).

4. Jane G. Haigh, *King Con: The Soapy Smith Story* (Whitehorse, YT: Wolf Creek Books, 2006).

5. Both Black and DeGraf wrote memoirs. See Martha Black, *My Ninety Years*, ed. Florence Whyard (Anchorage: Alaska Northwest Publishing, 1976), and Anna DeGraf, *Pioneering on the Yukon, 1892–1917*, ed. Roger S. Brown (Hamden, CT: Archon Books, 1992).

6. See Mayer, *Klondike Women*, and Murphy and Haigh, *Gold Rush Women*.

7. Murphy and Haigh, *Gold Rush Women*.

8. Margaret Clark Shand and Ora M. Shand, *The Summit and Beyond* (Caldwell, Idaho: Caxton Printers, 1959).

9. Alice Rollins Crane, *Dawson Daily News*, "Golden Clean-Up Edition," January 1902, 65.

10. Bay Ryley, *Gold Diggers of the Klondike: Prostitution in Dawson City, Yukon, 1898–1908* (Winnipeg, Canada: Watson and Dwyer, 1997).

11. See *Ferguson's City Directory, 1901* (available at UAF, Dawson City Museum Library, or YA).

12. London's original Stewart River Cabin was found and dismantled, and the materials were divided. Half went to construct a replica in Dawson City, where his original carved name can be seen today; the other half went to the Jack London Cabin at Jack London Square, on the waterfront in Oakland, California.

13. The *Klondike Nugget* reported on the prospecting expedition of two men, Finne and Kagel, who had returned from the new district in September 1900. Finne had been in the district in 1898. Finne and Kagel staked claim No. 37 Above on the right fork of Clear Creek. See *Klondike Nugget* on microfilm, UAF or YA. There is also an index to the *Nugget*.

14. Claim No. 2 Above was staked on September 5 and transferred in late September in halves and quarters for $600 a half share. Claim No. 1 Below was staked on September 10 to L. E. Ritchie, who worked it through 1901 and then sold a half share for $1 in June 1902. The second quarter was sold in May 1903 for $800 to Mary Lowery and Maggie McNeil. As I read these old recorded notices in the Dawson Mining District Records, Dawson Mining Recorder, in Dawson City, I found it interesting that there were other women attempting to mine on this remote creek.

15. *Klondike Nugget*.

16. Linda E. T. MacDonald and Lynette R. Bleiler, eds., *Gold & Galena: A History of the Mayo District* (Mayo, YT: Mayo Historical Society, 1990).

17. Dawson Mining District Records, Dawson Mining Recorder, Dawson City, YT.

18. For more about Belinda, see Melanie Mayer and Robert D'Armond, *Staking Her Claim: The Life of Belinda Mulrooney, Klondike and Alaska Entrepreneur* (Athens, Ohio: Swallow Press/Ohio University Press, 2000).

19. This and following details are from the *Dawson Daily News*, "Golden Clean-Up Edition," January 1, 1902.

20. "Coffee and sinkers" (doughnuts) is from a sign pictured in a famous Klondike photograph, and the description is from *Dawson Daily News*, "Golden Clean-Up Edition.".

21. *Klondike Nugget*, December 14, 1901.

22. DeGraf, *Pioneering on the Yukon.*

CHAPTER 3: WALKING OUT

1. Clary (Craig) Dawson, City Postal Records, YA.

2. *Yukon Sun*, January 17, 1903.

3. According to a story in the *Daily Klondike Nugget*, Rampart's newspaper, the *Alaska Forum*, had announced on December 20 that the stampede to the Chena had left Rampart the previous Monday night.

4. *Klondike Nugget*, March 4, 1903.

5. Ibid.

6. For the story of corporate mining in the Yukon, see Lewis Green, *Gold Hustlers* (Anchorage: Alaska Northwest Publishing, 1977).

7. For the more bourgeois Dawson, see Laura Berton, *I Married the Klondike* (1954; repr., Toronto: McClelland and Stewart, 1972).

8. My account is taken from Wickersham's memoir, James Wickersham, *Old Yukon: Tales, Trails, and Trials* (St. Paul, MN: West Publishing, 1938). The original diaries are at the ASL and are also now available online.

9. Wickersham, *Old Yukon*, 46.

10. Ibid., 142–43.

11. Mayo had operated trading posts for the Alaska Commercial Company at various stations on the river since 1874. He and his wife, Margaret, a Koyukon Athabascan, had twelve children, the oldest of whom were grown with families of their own by 1903. See Claire Rudolf Murphy and Jane G. Haigh, *Gold Rush Women* (Seattle, WA: Alaska Northwest Books, 1997).

12. Josie Earp's memories of her days in Rampart are chronicled in Josephine Sarah Marcus Earp, *I Married Wyatt Earp*, collected and edited by Glenn G. Boyer (Tucson: University of Arizona Press, 1976). Although the book has attracted controversy, I consider it an accurate memoir of her time in Alaska. Also Rex Beach, *The Barrier* (New York: A. L. Burt, 1908). The barrier Beach referred to was race: the hero, an army lieutenant of southern origins, cannot bring himself to marry the "half-breed" daughter of the trader, a thinly disguised Al Mayo.

13. This is the story that Tom Gilmore told to Genevieve Parker, who interviewed him in Fairbanks for her master's thesis. See Parker, "Evolution of Mining

Methods in Alaska" (master's thesis, University of Alaska School of Mines, 1929).

14. James Wickersham, *The Fairbanks Miner*, vol. 1, no. 1 (May 1903); online version at Alaska State Library—Historical Collections, http://library.state .ak.us/hist/fulltext/ASL-MS0107-62-29.htm, accessed October 22, 2006. Most versions of this story state that they saw the steamer from the top of Pedro Dome, but the incident occurred before Pedro staked his namesake creek.

15. Chena was on unstable ground and eventually eroded into the Tanana River. Most of what was Chena extended from the state campground at the end of Chena Pump Road to the sandbar on the other side of the channel.

16. Fairbanks Mining Book 2, p. 294, No. 1459, MF Roll 171. Angus also filed in Fairbanks on August 28, 1904, on Beaver Creek, a tributary of the South Fork of the Chena River, see Fairbanks Mining Book 4, p. 82, No. 5119, MF Roll 172, and on Mascot Creek in Tolavana country, see Fairbanks Mining Book 5, p. 21, MF Roll 21. Fairbanks Mining District Records, State of Alaska Department of Natural Resources Recorder's Office, Fairbanks, Alaska.

17. *FDNM*, "Tanana Goldfields Edition," Fairbanks, Alaska, 1919.

CHAPTER 4: INTO KANTISHNA

1. James Wickersham, *Old Yukon: Tales, Trails, and Trials* (St. Paul, MN: West Publishing, 1938).

2. See Davis's story in Herbert Heller, *Sourdough Sagas: The Journals, Memoirs, Tales, and Recollections of the Earliest Alaskan Gold Miners, 1883–1923* (Cleveland, OH: World Publishing, 1967).

3. Alfred Hulse Brooks, *Blazing Alaska's Trails* (Fairbanks: University of Alaska Press, 1973).

4. Wickersham, *Old Yukon*. The transliterations are Wickersham's.

5. Ibid., 223.

6. Ibid., 269, 284, 291.

7. Grant Pearson, with Philip Newell, *My Life of High Adventure* (Englewood Cliffs, NJ: Prentice Hall, 1962), 54.

8. According to Pearson, they "set out after the holidays in 1905." See Grant Pearson, "Joe Quigley, Sourdough," *Alaska Sportsman Magazine*, March 1950, 14, and Pearson, *My Life of High Adventure*, 54.

9. Pearson, "Joe Quigley."

10. The name of the river and the mining district is Fortymile; Forty Mile is the name of the historical townsite. See Mike Gates, *Gold at Fortymile Creek* (Vancouver: UBC Press, 1994).

11. Fairbanks Mining District, MF Roll 172, Book 5, p. 33. Fairbanks Mining District Records, State of Alaska Department of Natural Resources Recorder's Office, Fairbanks, Alaska.

12. Many of Joe's claims were actually located in December 1904, apparently just before he and Horn set out for the Kantishna. MF Roll 172, No. 1 Above

Jump Off Joe Creek, Fairbanks Book 5, p. 33; No. 2 Below Fourth of July Creek, Fairbanks Book 5, p. 34, with L. J. English, and John L. Lee. Fairbanks Mining District Records, State of Alaska Department of Natural Resources Recorder's Office, Fairbanks, Alaska.

13. The earliest claims in the Kantishna area are recorded in the Fairbanks Mining District record books, available now on microfilm, Fairbanks Mining District Records, State of Alaska Department of Natural Resources Recorder's Office, Fairbanks, Alaska.

14. Pearson, "Joe Quigley."

15. *Fairbanks Weekly News,* August 24, 1905.

16. *Fairbanks Evening News,* August 24, 1905.

17. *Fairbanks Weekly News,* August 9, 1905.

18. Ibid., September 25, 1905.

19. Fairbanks Mining District record books, Fairbanks Claims, MF Roll 172, Book 4, p. 82. Fairbanks Mining District Records, State of Alaska Department of Natural Resources Recorder's Office, Fairbanks, Alaska.

20. *Fairbanks Weekly News,* August 17, 1906.

21. *Fairbanks Evening News,* August 25, 1906.

22. Ibid., September 10, 1906.

23. Ibid., August 27, 1906.

24. For more about dredging, see David Neufeld and Patrick Habiluk, *Make It Pay! Gold Dredge #4* (Klondike, Yukon, Canada: Kegley Books, 1994), and Green, *The Gold Hustlers.*

CHAPTER 5: DIGGING IN

1. Map and notes are in the USGS-APU; photographs are in the Stephen Capps Photo Collection, UAF.

2. Since that early trip, the Park Service has restored Fannie's house near the airstrip as a historical exhibit.

3. The smallest tributary creeks were commonly referred to as pups.

4. Stephen R. Capps, *The Kantishna Region,* Alaska USGS Bulletin 687 (Washington, DC: U.S. Government Printing Office, 1919).

5. Ibid.

CHAPTER 6: HARD ROCK

1. Charles Sheldon Collection, UAF.

2. For example, see JoAnne Wold, "Fannie the Hike," in *The Way It Was* (Anchorage: Alaska Northwest Publishing, 1988), 45.

3. *Nenana News,* January 19, 1918, 2.

4. *Fairbanks Daily Times,* January 5, 1910, and March 29, 1910.

5. Fairbanks court records, State of Alaska Archives, Juneau. For more about Belinda, see Melanie Mayer and Robert D'Armond, *Staking Her Claim: The Life of Belinda Mulrooney, Klondike and Alaska Entrepreneur* (Athens, Ohio: Swallow Press/Ohio University Press, 2000).

6. Letter, Fannie McKenzie to Charles Sheldon, Charles Sheldon Collection, UAF.

7. See Ed Brooker reminiscences, NPS-DENA.

8. Clara Rust Papers, Box 9, Ledger Book, p. 52, "First Memberships," Charter Roll #72, February 19, 1916, UAF Archives.

9. Letter, Fannie McKenzie to Charles Sheldon, Charles Sheldon Collection, UAF.

10. Stephen R. Capps, *The Kantishna Region*, Alaska USGS Bulletin 687 (Washington, DC: U.S. Government Printing Office, 1919).

11. *Nenana News*, February 25 and February 28, 1919.

12. Mayo Historical Society, *Gold and Galena* (Mayo, Yukon, Canada: Mayo Historical Society, 1990).

13. *Nenana News*, September 8, 1919.

14. Ibid., October 10, 1919.

15. Ibid., May 14, 1920.

16. Ibid., May 1, 1920.

17. Ibid., May 3, 1920.

18. Photograph, taken after 1918, Fannie Quigley Collection, UAF Archives. I have never found any written confirmation of Fannie's presence in Nenana at that time.

19. *Nenana News*, June 14, 1920.

20. Ibid., September 26, 1919.

21. Ibid., July 19, 1920.

22. Ibid., August 17, 1920.

23. Ibid., February 24, 1921.

24. Rolfe Buzzell, "Lode Mining on Quigley Ridge and in the Glacier Peak Area," unpublished report of the National Park Service, May 4, 1988, 8. NPS-DENA

25. Ibid., 9.

26. Letter, author's collection.

27. Letter, Fannie to her sister, March 23, 1923, author's collection, courtesy of descendants.

28. Ruth Carson, "Joe and Fannie Quigley," *Alaska Magazine*, April 1970.

CHAPTER 7: WILDERNESS LIFE

1. Belmore Browne, "Hitting the Home Trail from Mt. McKinley," *Outing Magazine* 62, no. 4 (July 1913): 387–401.

2. Fannie McKenzie to Mary McLain, August 20, 1923; Fannie McKenzie to Mary McLain, March 23, 1923. I have retained the original wording and spelling in these letters. Courtesy Oien family.

3. Grant Pearson, with Philip Newell, *My Life of High Adventure* (Englewood Cliffs, NJ: Prentice Hall, 1962), 55.

4. Ibid.

5. Lois McGarvey, *Along Alaska Trails* (New York: Vantage Press, 1960), 74.

6. Browne, "Hitting the Home Trail," 398–400.

7. Stephen Capps, photo, Stephen Capps Collection, UAF.

8. Stephen Capps, field notes, USGS-APU.

9. Ibid.

10. Fannie McKenzie to Charles Sheldon, copy in Charles Sheldon Collection, UAF. An additional notation on the Capps map verifies a Quigley cabin located on the top of the ridge.

11. Mary Lee Davis, *We Are Alaskans* (Boston: Wilde, 1931); letter to sister Mary, February 2, 1928, courtesy Oien family.

12. Fannie McKenzie to her sister, mailed from Chena, August 1907; Davis, *We Are Alaskans*, 213.

13. Stephen R. Capps, *The Kantishna Region*, Alaska USGS Bulletin 687 (Washington, DC: U.S. Government Printing Office, 1919).

14. Ira B. Joralemon, *Adventure Beacons* (New York: Society of Mining Engineers of AIME for the Mining and Metallurgical Society of America, 1976), 309. I thank Chuck Hawley for bringing this work to my attention.

15. Marie Rosický, *Bohemian-American Cookbook: An English Translation of the Cook Book Published in the Bohemian Language and Compiled by Marie Rosický* (Omaha, NE: Automatic Printing, 1949). The copy I have is a comb-bound version, from the seventh printing.

16. Ibid.

17. Ibid.

18. Letter to sister Mary McLain, March 23, 1923, courtesy Oien family.

19. Pearson, *My Life of High Adventure*.

20. McGarvey, *Along Alaska Trails*, 78.

21. Virgil Burford, *North to Danger* (New York: John Day, 1950), 228.

22. Ibid.

CHAPTER 8: THE OUTDOOR LIFE

1. Letter, Fannie McKenzie to her sister Mary McLain, August 1907, courtesy Oien family.

2. Charles Sheldon, *Wilderness of Denali* (New York: Charles Scribner's, 1930).

3. Grinnell and Roosevelt quoted in C. Hart Merriam's "Introduction," in ibid.

4. Quoted in James B. Trefethan, *An American Crusade for Wildlife* (Alexandria, VA: Boone and Crockett Club, 1975), 192.

5. For Karstens's opinion, see Charles Sheldon Collection, UAF, and William E. Brown, *Denali: Symbol of the Alaskan Wild* (Virginia Beach, VA: Donning, 1993), introduction, available online as *A History of the Denali–Mount McKinley Region, Alaska* at http://www.cr.nps.gov/history/online_books/dena/hrs7b.htm (accessed September 25, 2006)

6. Sheldon Diary, Charles Sheldon Collection, August 4, 1907, UAF. In *Wilderness of Denali*, which was not published until 1930, following his death, Sheldon said that they "passed the night in the hospitable cabin of Joe and Fannie Quigley," 111. Perhaps he felt the need to accommodate more modern sensibilities on the East Coast when he referred to her as Fannie Quigley, or perhaps by the time he edited for publication, she *was* Fannie Quigley.

7. See photo.

8. Merriam, "Introduction."

9. Sheldon, *Wilderness of Denali*, 294–95.

10. Ibid., 294.

11. Ibid., 296.

12. Belmore Browne, "Hitting the Home Trail from Mt. McKinley," *Outing Magazine* 62, no. 4 (July 1913): 398–400.

13. I am indebted to Susan Kollin for this analysis. See Kollin, *Nature's State: Imagining Alaska as the Last Frontier* (Chapel Hill: University of North Carolina Press, 2001), 49.

14. Phyllis Demuth Movius, "The Role of Women in the Founding and Development of Fairbanks, Alaska, 1903–1923" (master's thesis, University of Alaska Fairbanks, 1996), 61–62.

15. *Alaska Dispatch*, April 23, 1920. I thank Mike Burwell for passing this along. Ruth, the young widow, later married Fairbanks businessman James Barrack, whom she met on the trip to Alaska. "Ruth Barrack—Long Time UA Supporter," University of Alaska "Info," available online at http://www.alaska.edu/opa/eInfo/index.xml?StoryID=302 (accessed June 1, 2005).

16. Lois McGarvey, *Along Alaska Trails* (New York: Vantage Press, 1960), 78. I thank Candy Waugaman for bringing Lois's book to my attention.

17. Ibid.

18. Selling the furs directly to tourists in Fairbanks and later to buyers in Los Angeles, Lois made a fair living until the Depression in 1929.

19. Mary Lee Davis, *We Are Alaskans* (Boston: Wilde, 1931). The date of her trip is established in notes from Denali National Park, Cultural Resources Department, Denali Park, Alaska. Use of horses, ibid., 182.

20. Ibid., 197.

21. Ibid.

22. It is impossible to know if this and the following statements presented by Mary Lee Davis as quotes from Fannie are, in fact, direct quotes. I suspect that

they were written by Davis from remembered conversations or from notes she had taken during her talks with Fannie.

23. Ibid.

24. Ibid., 210.

25. Ibid.

26. Ibid., 204–5.

27. Ibid.

28. Ibid., 211, quoting Fannie. Of course, it is impossible to know how accurately Davis quoted Fannie.

29. Grant Pearson, with Philip Newell, *My Life of High Adventure* (Englewood Cliffs, NJ: Prentice Hall, 1962), 55; and Grant Pearson, "Fannie Quigley, Fronterswoman," *Alaska Sportsman*, August 1947, 31.

30. Ibid.

31. Ibid.

32. Davis, *We Are Alaskans*, 209.

33. Letter, Fannie Quigley to Mary McLain and sons, February 2, 1928.

CHAPTER 9: WILDERNESS VISITORS

1. Gail Bederman, *Manliness & Civilization: A Cultural History of Gender and Race in the United States, 1880–1917* (Chicago: University of Chicago Press, 1995), 125, 127.

2. Roderick Nash, *Wilderness and the American Mind* (New Haven, CT: Yale University Press, 1982), 275.

3. Richard White, "Are You an Environmentalist or Do You Work for a Living?" in *Uncommon Ground*, ed. William Cronon (New York: Norton, 1995), 172.

4. Fannie Quigley to Teresa Oien, November 3, 1929.

5. Susan Kollin, *Nature's State: Imagining Alaska as the Last Frontier* (Chapel Hill: University of North Carolina, 2001), 49.

6. Ibid., 94.

7. Lois McGarvey, *Along Alaska Trails* (New York: Vantage Press, 1960), 74.

8. Ibid.

9. Ibid.

10. For biographical information about Mary Lee Davis, I am grateful to Phyllis Demuth Movius, "The Role of Women in the Founding and Development of Fairbanks, Alaska, 1903–1923" (master's thesis, University of Alaska Fairbanks, 1996). The exact dates of the Davis's trip are ambiguous.

11. Mary Lee Davis, *We Are Alaskans* (Boston: Wilde, 1931), 199.

12. McGarvey, *Along Alaska Trails*, 76.

13. Davis, *We Are Alaskans*, 199, 208.

14. Ibid., 206.

15. Mrs. Nannie Biddle to Viljalmer Steffanson, Staffanson Collection, Dartmouth Library, Dartmouth College, Hanover, NH.

16. I found the *Pittsburgh Press* article on Mrs. Biddle in the Fannie Quigley Collection in the UAF Archives (undated fragment). The details of the story were confirmed in *New York Times* articles on December 2, 1931; January 2, 1932; January 17, 1932, 5, c2; March 22, 1932, 4; and in *FDNM* articles on January 1, 1932; January 15, 1932; March 21, 1932, 4; March 26, 1932, 7; April 5, 1932, 4; and April 6, 1932, 5.

17. *New York Times*, October 3, 1933, and October 18, 1933, 11, c2.

18. William E. Brown, *Denali: Symbol of the Alaskan Wild* (Virginia Beach, VA: Donning, 1993), 90–94, a management history available online as *A History of the Denali–Mount McKinley Region, Alaska* at http://www.cr.nps.gov/history/online_books/dena/hrs7b.htm (accessed September 25, 2006); House Subcommittee of the Committee on Public Lands, *Hearing on a Bill to Establish Mount McKinley National Park*, 64th Cong., 1st sess., May 4, 1916.

19. The booklet's text is appended to the committee testimony in the *Congressional Record*.

20. House Subcommittee, *Hearing on Mount McKinley National Park*. For further information on park history, see Brown, *Denali: Symbol*.

21. Grant Pearson, with Philip Newell, *My Life of High Adventure* (Englewood Cliffs, NJ: Prentice Hall, 1962).

22. Original work on the history of the Park Road was done by Gail Evans, "From Myth to Reality: Travel Experiences and Landscape Perceptions in the Shadow of Mt. McKinley, Alaska, 1876–1938" (master's thesis, University of California—Santa Barbara, 1987).

23. In fact, the miners were prescient: mining access through the park has caused continual conflict.

24. *FDNM*, July 22, 1930.

25. The annual report for 1932 noted, "An extension of approximately 22 miles, to Wonder Lake is contemplated. From this point an excellent view of the mountain is afforded." NPS-DENA.

CHAPTER 10: SELLING OUT

1. Fannie Quigley to Teresa Oien, Kantishna, Alaska, November 3, 1929, courtesy of Oien family.

2. *FDNM*, June 2, 1930.

3. Mary Lee Davis, *We Are Alaskans* (Boston: Wilde, 1931), 213.

4. *FDNM*, September 10, 1930.

5. Davis, *We Are Alaskans*, 213.

6. *FDNM*, March 28, 1931.

7. A. D. McCrae had made a fortune in Saskatchewan Land and the Fraser River Lumber Company. He built a thirty-room mansion, Hycroft, in Vancouver in 1909, which was the social hub of upper-class society in the city before World War II. St. Georges School, BC, available online at http://www

.stgeorges.bc.ca/marker/main/hycroft/fullreport.html (accessed September 25, 2006).

8. Ira B. Joralemon, *Adventure Beacons* (New York: Society of Mining Engineers of AIME for the Mining and Metallurgical Society of America, 1976), 304–11. Thanks to Chuck Hawley for alerting me to this source.

9. Ibid.

10. Ibid.

11. Ibid., 308.

12. Ibid., 310. Also *FDNM*, September 19, 1931, and November 7, 1933.

13. Joralemon, *Adventure Beacons*, 310–11, and *FDNM*, July 13, 1934. Joralemon described the tunnel as into the Little Annie claim, but the *News-Miner* referred to it as the Red Top. Ibid.

14. *Alaska Weekly*, December 21, 1934; also *FDNM*, December 3, 1934, and December 21, 1934.

15. *FDNM*, March 1, 1934.

16. One of Alaska's most famous mining men, W. E. Dunkle, developed the Golden Zone Mine (GZM) in a similar fashion with Anchorage investors in 1938, after being turned down by the bigger companies. GZM was chartered as a public stock corporation in May 1938. See Charles Caldwell Hawley, *Wesley Earl Dunkle: Alaska's Flying Miner* (Boulder: University Press of Colorado, 2003), 154.

17. *FDNM*, "Goldfields Edition," November 29, 1936, Quartz section, 3, 5.

18. Ibid.

19. The company was named after one of Quigley's original claims on the south side of Quigley Ridge, generating some modern confusion. After further exploration of the Little Annie vein system, they abandoned it and focused exclusively on the Banjo claim after 1936. Claims transferred to E. Fransen and C. M. Hawkins included the Silver Pick, Little Annie Lode, Little Annie Lode #2, Frances, Martha Q, Golden Eagle, Gold Dollar, Lucky Strike, Sulpher Lode, Water Level, White Hawk, Red Top, Darling, and Polly Wonder, as well as an undivided two-thirds interest in Pennsylvania, Keystone, and Pittsburgh. See *FDNM*, "Goldfields Edition."

20. *FDNM*, "Goldfields Edition," November 29, 1936.

21. Ibid., sec. 1, p. 3, and Quartz section.

22. Ibid., Quartz section, 5.

CHAPTER 11: DRIFTING APART

1. Ira B. Joralemon, *Adventure Beacons* (New York: Society of Mining Engineers of AIME for the Mining and Metallurgical Society of America, 1976), 308.

2. Mary Lee Davis, *We Are Alaskans* (Boston: Wilde, 1931), 199.

3. Lois McGarvey, *Along Alaska's Trails* (New York: Vantage Press, 1960), 76.

4. Joralemon, *Adventure Beacons*, 306.

5. Ibid., 310; also *FDNM*, September 19, 1931, and November 7, 1933.

6. Joralemon, *Adventure Beacons*, 310.

7. *Alaska Weekly*, December 21, 1934; also *FDNM*, December 3, 1934, and December 21, 1934.

8. *FDNM*, December 3, 1934, and July 18, 1935; *Alaska Weekly*, December 21, 1934.

9. *FDNM*, January 10, 1936, 8; January 11, 1936, 8; and February 15, 1936, 4.

10. Pat Eagan Franklin was that little girl. She had contracted scarlet fever after being operated on for appendicitis and spent months in the hospital; her story is well known in Fairbanks. Personal communication with the author.

11. State of Alaska Probate Records.

12. Grant Pearson, "Fannie Quigley, Frontierswoman," *Alaska Sportsman Magazine*, August 1947, 32.

13. Grant Pearson, "Joe Quigley, Sourdough," *Alaska Sportsman Magazine*, March 1950, 28. Joe died November 23, 1958, in a Seattle rest home at age eighty-nine.

14. *FDNM*, November 2, 1938: "New camp buildings have been put up by George Bachner, Fairbanks contractor, who has a small crew at the mine." In a personal communication, a Bachner family member also said that Bachner built the Moose Creek building. In another personal communication, Magdalene Cassidy testified as to the date.

15. *FDNM*, December 31, 1937.

16. Jim Hutchison oral history tape, as related by William F. Schneider, Oral History Collection, UAF.

17. Grant Pearson, with Philip Newell, *My Life of High Adventure* (Englewood Cliffs, NJ: Prentice Hall, 1962), 59–60.

18. The death of a young drifter, chronicled by Jon Krakauer in *Into the Wild* (New York: Doubleday, 2000), took place less than 50 miles from Kantishna and on Fannie's route home from Nenana.

19. Virgil Burford, *North to Danger* (New York: John Day, 1950).

20. Major George Hall, *Some Time Again* (Seattle, WA: Superior Publishing, 1945).

21. Ibid., 117.

22. Ibid., 125–26.

23. Ibid.

EPILOGUE

1. This report on Fannie's funeral appeared in *FDNM*, September 2, 1944.

2. Bay Ryley presented this idea at the 1992 "Women in the North" conference in Fairbanks. See her *Gold Diggers of the Klondike* (Winnipeg, Canada: Watson and Dwyer Publishing, 1997).

3. Melanie Mayer, *Klondike Women: True Tales of the 1897–98 Gold Rush* (Athens, Ohio: Swallow Press/Ohio University Press, 1989); Francis Backhouse, *Women of the Goldrush* (Vancouver, BC: Whitecap Books, 2000); Sally Zanjani, *A Mine of Her Own* (Lincoln: University of Nebraska Press, 1997); Claire Rudolf Murphy and Jane G. Haigh, *Gold Rush Women* (Seattle, WA: Alaska Northwest Books, 1977).

4. *FDNM*, June 5, 1930. Harry Myers, editor of the Lapeer County Press, had stopped by while visiting his son, a park ranger, establishing the connection with the Quigleys.

5. Jim Hutchison oral history tape, as related by William F. Schneider, Oral History Collection, UAF.

6. Grant Pearson, with Philip Newell, *My Life of High Adventure* (Englewood Cliffs, NJ: Prentice Hall, 1962), 59–60.

7. Ibid., and Grant Pearson, "Fannie Quigley, Frontierswoman," *Alaska Sportsman Magazine*, August 1947.

8. *FDNM*, September 2, 1944.

BIBLIOGRAPHY

—w—

PRIMARY SOURCES

Books

Burford, Virgil. *North to Danger*. New York: John Day, 1950.

Davis, Mary Lee. *We Are Alaskans*. Boston: Wilde, 1931.

Ferguson, Maria L. *Dawson City, Yukon Territory and Alaska Directory and Gazetteer, 1901*. Dawson City, YT: Maria L. Ferguson, 1901.

Hall, George. *Some Time Again*. Seattle, WA: Superior Publishing, 1945.

Joralmon, Ira B. *Adventure Beacons*. New York: Society of Mining Engineers of AIME for the Mining and Metallurgical Society of America, 1976.

McGarvey, Lois. *Along Alaska Trails*. New York: Vantage Press, 1960.

Pearson, Grant H., with Philip Newell. *My Life of High Adventure*. Englewood Cliffs, NJ: Prentice Hall, 1962.

Sheldon, Charles. *Wilderness of the Upper Yukon*. New York: Charles Scribner's, 1908.

———. *Wilderness of Denali*. New York: Charles Scribner's, 1930.

Wickersham, James. *Old Yukon: Tales, Trails and Trials*. St. Paul, MN: West Publishing, 1930.

Articles

Browne, Belmore. "Hitting the Home Trail from Mt. McKinley." *Outing Magazine* 62, no. 4, July 1913.

Carson, Ruth. "Joe and Fannie Quigley." *Alaska Magazine*, April 1970.

Crane, Alice Rollins. *Dawson Daily News*, "Golden Clean-Up Edition," January 1902.

Pearson, Grant. "Fannie Quigley, Frontierswoman." *Alaska Sportsman Magazine*, August 1947.

———. "Joe Quigley, Sourdough." *Alaska Sportsman Magazine*, March 1950.

Government Publications

Capps, Stephen. *The Kantishna Region Alaska*. USGS Bulletin 687. Washington, DC: U.S. Government Printing Office, 1919.

U.S. Congress. House Subcommittee of the Committee on Public Lands. *Hearing on a Bill to Establish Mount McKinley National Park*. 64th Cong., 1st sess., May 4, 1916.

Archival and Manuscript Materials

Brooker, Ed, reminiscences. NPS-DENA.

Capps, Stephen, Collection. UAF.

Capps, Stephen. Field notes. USGS-APU.

Dawson Mining District Records. Dawson Mining Recorder, Dawson City, Yukon.

Fairbanks Mining District Records. State of Alaska Department of Natural Resources Recorder's Office, Fairbanks, Alaska.

Foster, Stephen, Collection. UAF.

Kantishna Mining District Records. State of Alaska Department of Natural Resources Recorder's Office, Fairbanks, Alaska.

Quigley, Fannie, Collection. UAF.

Rust, Clara, Papers. UAF.

Sheldon, Charles, Collection. UAF.

Wickersham, James. *The Fairbanks Miner*, vol. 1, no. 1 (May 1903); online version at Alaska State Library—Historical Collections, http://library.state.ak.us/hist/fulltext/ASL-MS0107-62-29.htm, accessed October 22, 2006.

Periodicals

Alaska Dispatch (Seattle, WA)

Alaska Forum (Rampart, AK)

Alaska Weekly (Seattle, WA)

Dawson Daily News (Dawson City, YT)

Dawson Daily News, "Golden Clean-Up Edition," January 1, 1902

Fairbanks Daily News-Miner (Fairbanks, AK)

Fairbanks Daily News-Miner, "Goldfields Edition," November 29, 1936

Fairbanks Daily Times (Fairbanks, AK)

Fairbanks Evening News (Fairbanks, AK)

Fairbanks Weekly News (Fairbanks, AK)

Klondike Nugget (Dawson City, YT)

Nenana News (Nenana, AK)

Yukon Sun (Dawson City, YT)

SECONDARY SOURCES

Aldrich, Bess Streeter. *A Lantern in Her Hand*. 1928. Reprint, New York: New American Library, 1989.

Beach, Rex. *The Barrier*. New York: A. L. Burt, 1908.

Bederman, Gail. *Manliness & Civilization: A Cultural History of Gender and Race in the United States, 1880–1917*. Chicago: University of Chicago Press, 1995.

Berton, Laura. *I Married the Klondike*. 1954. Reprint, Toronto: McClelland and Stewart, 1972.

Black, Martha. *My Ninety Years*. Edited by Florence Whyard. Anchorage: Alaska Northwest Publishing, 1976.

Bogue, Alan. *Money at Interest: The Farm Mortgage on the Middle Border*. Lincoln: University of Nebraska Press, 1969.

Brown, Chip. "Call of the Wild." Review of *Going to Extremes*, by Joe McGinnis. *Washington Post*, September 14, 1980.

Brown, William E. *Denali: Symbol of the Alaskan Wild*. Denali National Park Alaska, Alaska Natural History Association, and Virginia Beach, VA: Donning, 1993.

Bundtzen, Thomas K. "A History of Mining in the Kantishna Hills." *Alaska Journal*, Spring 1978, 150–61.

Buzzell, Rolfe. "Lode Mining on Quigley Ridge and in the Glacier Peak Area." National Park Service Report, May 4, 1988.

Capek, Thomas. *The Czechs in America*. New York: Houghton Mifflin, 1920.

Cather, Willa. *My Ántonia*. New York: Houghton Mifflin, 1954.

Creighton, Dorothy. *Nebraska: A History*. Louisville, KY: AASLH, 1977.

Cronon, William. "The Trouble with Wilderness, or Getting Back to the Wrong Nature." In *Uncommon Ground*, edited by William Cronon, 69–90. New York: Norton, 1995.

DeGraf, Anna. *Pioneering on the Yukon, 1892–1917*. Edited by Roger S. Brown. Hamden, CT: Archon Books, 1992.

Earp, Josephine Sarah Marcus. *I Married Wyatt Earp*. Collected and edited by Glenn G. Boyer. Tucson: University of Arizona Press, 1976.

Evans, Gail. "From Myth to Reality: Travel Experiences and Landscape Perceptions in the Shadow of Mt. McKinley, Alaska, 1876–1938." Master's thesis, University of California Santa Barbara, 1987.

Farragher, John Mack. *Sugar Creek: Life on the Illinois Prairie*. New Haven, CT: Yale University Press, 1986.

Gates, Michael. *Gold at Fortymile Creek*. Vancouver: UBC Press, 1994.

Grant, Madison. "The Establishment of Mt. McKinley Park." In *Hunting and Conservation: The Book of the Boone and Crockett Club*, edited by George B. Grinnell and Charles Sheldon. New Haven, CT: Yale University Press, 1925.

Green, Lewis. *Gold Hustlers*. Anchorage: Alaska Northwest Publishing, 1977.

Grinnell, George B., and Charles Sheldon, eds. *Hunting and Conservation: The Book of the Boone and Crockett Club*. New Haven, CT: Yale University Press, 1925.

Haigh, Jane G. *King Con: The Story of Soapy Smith*. Whitehorse, YT: Friday 501 Books, 2006.

Hawley, Charles Caldwell. *Wesley Earl Dunkle: Alaska's Flying Miner.* Boulder: University Press of Colorado, 2003.

Heller, Herbert. *Sourdough Sagas: The Journals, Memoirs, Tales, and Recollections of the Earliest Alaskan Gold Miners, 1883–1923.* Cleveland, OH: World Publishing, 1967.

Herman, Daniel Justin. *Hunting and the American Imagination.* Washington, DC: Smithsonian Institution Press, 2001.

Jacoby, Karl. *Crimes against Nature: Squatters, Poachers, Thieves and the Hidden History of American Conservation.* Berkeley: University of California Press, 2001.

Kelcey, Barbara. "Lost in the Rush: The Forgotten Women of the Klondike Stampede." Master's thesis, University of Victoria, 1989.

Klein, Maury. *Birth of the Union Pacific.* Garden City, NY: Doubleday, 1987.

Kollin, Susan. *Nature's State: Imagining Alaska as the Last Frontier.* Chapel Hill: University of North Carolina Press, 2001.

Kolodny, Annette. *The Land before Her: Fantasy and Experience of the American Frontiers, 1630–1860.* Chapel Hill: University of North Carolina Press, 1984.

MacDonald, Linda E. T., and Lynette R. Bleiler, eds. *Gold & Galena: A History of the Mayo District.* Mayo, YT: Mayo Historical Society, 1990.

Marshall, Robert. *Arctic Village.* 1933. Reprint, Fairbanks: University of Alaska Press, 1991.

Mayer, Melanie J. *Klondike Women: True Tales of the 1897–1898 Gold Rush.* Athens, Ohio: Swallow Press/Ohio University Press, 1989.

Mayer, Melanie, and Robert D'Armond. *Staking Her Claim: The Life of Belinda Mulrooney, Klondike and Alaska Entrepreneur.* Athens, Ohio: Swallow Press/Ohio University Press, 2000.

McPhee, John. *Coming into the Country.* New York: Noonday Press, 1977.

Movius, Phyllis Demuth. "The Role of Women in the Founding and Development of Fairbanks, Alaska, 1903–1923." Master's thesis, University of Alaska Fairbanks, 1996.

Murphy, Claire Rudolf, and Jane G. Haigh. *Gold Rush Women.* Seattle, WA: Alaska Northwest Books, 1997.

Nash, Roderick. *Wilderness and the American Mind.* New Haven, CT: Yale University Press, 1967.

Olson, James C. *History of Nebraska.* Lincoln: University of Nebraska Press, 1966.

Parker, Genevieve. "Evolution of Mining Methods in Alaska." Master's thesis, University of Alaska School of Mines, 1929.

People of Saunders County, Nebraska. *Saunders County History.* Wahoo, NE: Saunders County Historical Society, 1983.

Reiger, John F. *American Sportsmen and the Origins of Conservation.* Norman: University of Oklahoma Press, 1975.

Rosický, Marie. *Bohemian-American Cookbook: An English Translation of the Cook Book Published in the Bohemian Language and Compiled by Marie Rosický*. Omaha: Automatic Printing, 1949.

Rosicky, Rose. *A History of Czechs in Nebraska*. Omaha: Czech Historical Society of Nebraska, 1929.

Ryley, Bay. *Gold Diggers of the Klondike: Prostitution in Dawson City, Yukon, 1898–1908*. Winnipeg: Watson and Dwyer, 1997.

Sherwood, Morgan B. *Big Game in Alaska: A History of Wildlife and People*. New Haven, CT: Yale University Press, 1961.

Slotkin, Richard. *The Fatal Environment: The Myth of the Frontier in the Age of Industrialization, 1800–1890*. New York: Atheneum, 1985.

———. *Gunfighter Nation: The Myth of the Frontier in Twentieth-Century America*. New York: HarperPerrenial, 1993.

Trefethan, James B. *An American Crusade for Wildlife*. Alexandria, VA: Boone and Crockett Club, 1975.

Warren, Louis. *The Hunters Game: Poachers and Conservationists in Twentieth-Century America*. New Haven, CT: Yale University Press, 1997.

Webb, Melody. *Yukon, the Last Frontier*. Lincoln: University of Nebraska Press, 1985.

White, Richard. *It's Your Misfortune but None of My Own*. Norman: University of Oklahoma Press, 1991.

———. "Are You an Environmentalist or Do You Work for a Living? Work and Nature." In *Uncommon Ground: Toward Re-inventing Nature,* edited by William Cronon, 171–86. New York: Norton, 1996.

Wold, JoAnne. "Fannie the Hike." In *The Way It Was*. Anchorage: Northwest Publishing, 1988.

Zanjani, Sally. *A Mine of Her Own: Women Prospectors in the American West, 1850–1950*. Lincoln: University of Nebraska Press, 1997.

INDEX

—⚭—

Page numbers in italics indicate illustrations.